LINCOLN
A Pictorial History

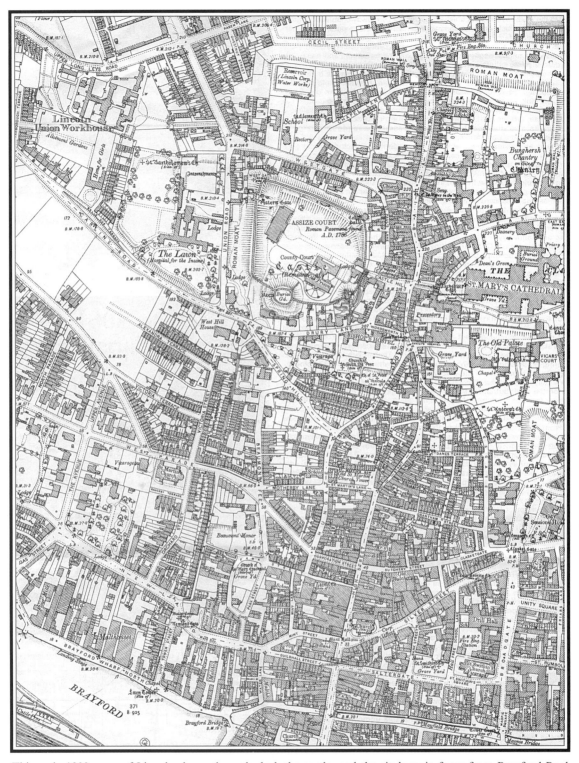

This early 1900s map of Lincoln shows the cathedral, the castle, and the city's main focus from Brayford Pool northwards. Note particularly the size of the workhouse (upper left-hand corner) which was known as the Burton Road Institution in the early 1900s. It stood on Upper Long Leys Road, backing onto the Lawn Hospital; the site of the workhouse is now occupied by a new housing estate. Union Road nearby gives us a clue as to its whereabouts.

LINCOLN
A Pictorial History

Ann Yeates-Langley

Phillimore

1997

Published by
PHILLIMORE & CO. LTD.,
Shopwyke Manor Barn, Chichester, West Sussex

ISBN 1 86077 059 2

Printed and bound in Great Britain by
BIDDLES LTD.
Guildford, Surrey

List of Illustrations

Frontispiece: Map of central Lincoln, early 1900s

Acknowledgements

I wish to thank all the following people who have kindly loaned me their photographs, postcards and reproductions: Eric Croft, 14, 47, 55, 58, 61, 62, 70, 75, 77-9, 83, 84, 95-9, 101, 104, 113, 115, 117, 118, 121, 123-5, 127-31, 134-6, 145-50, 152, 172, 173; D.S. Glover, 28, 114; John Hinman, 100, 126, 137, 151, 153-61; Richard Groves, 3, 4, 17, 20, 22, 29, 32, 36, 38, 45, 51, 56, 132, 133; Ray Hooley, 138-43, 166-70; R.A. Johnson, Kamara, 57, 122, 179, 182; Michael Jones, 6, 10, 13; *Lincoln Echo*, 60, 164, 174, 175; Lincolnshire Standard Group, 20, 23, 178; May Martin, 165; T. Sutton, 19; Rebecca Umney, 5; David Vale, 1, 7, 8, 12, 65; Ann Yeates-Langley, 2, 16, 18, 24-6, 33, 34, 39, 40, 46, 48-50, 52, 64, 80, 116, 177, 181.

I would also like to thank Michael Jones, Director, Lincoln Archaeology and Neil Wright, Industrial Archaeologist, for checking the material, and also David Vale for loaning his reproductions of a variety of periods of Lincoln's history. Eric Croft and Richard Groves generously lent me postcards from their collections and John Hinman lent me his Panoramic Views of Lincoln taken in the 1930s, which have greatly added to the interest. Caroline Mattock has assisted me in the preparation of the index.

I would also like to thank Lincoln Co-operative Society for allowing me to reproduce photographs from the history of the Society. The following photographs were reproduced from the Local Studies Collection, Lincoln Central Library by courtesy of Lincolnshire County Council, Education and Cultural Services Directorate. Thanks to Lincoln Library staff for their courtesy and help: 9, 11, 37, 42, 44, 52, 54, 59, 60, 63, 68, 69, 71-4, 76, 81, 82, 85, 86, 102, 103, 105-111, 119, 120, 144, 162, 164, 174, 175.

Dedicated to
Oliver, Rebecca and all my friends in Lincoln.

Introduction

Lincoln is a city well loved by most people who have the privilege to live there or to visit it. Visually it is a dramatic city, perhaps unique because it has not become surrounded by enormous suburbs that have drastically changed the layout that originated with the Romans. As it spreads over the hillside the visual impact cannot fail to stir. I share with others a special feeling of coming home when I see the cathedral and Ellis's mill illuminated at night on top of the hill. Over many decades people have been recording the city: either in engravings and paintings, or by photography, on film and video. It has inspired engravers such as Buck and Grimm; artists such as Turner, De Wint, Lowery, and David Vale for his reconstructions of life in times past. Local photographers such as Slingsby, Gadsby, Draper and Moreland have recorded life in Lincoln; the earliest records show studios operating from 1867.

One of the best approaches to Lincoln is by the relief road, then via the Carholme Road, alongside the old racecourse, another evocative reminder of Lincoln's history. From the relief road one can clearly see the ridge that is the ancient Jurassic Way that went north-south through Lincolnshire, as a result of glacial action many thousands of years previously. This action formed a gap about two miles wide which allowed the River Till and the River Witham to surge through, eventually creating the Brayford Pool where the two rivers meet. Our story begins and ends with the Brayford Pool where the first settlers lived; iron-age conical huts have been found. These people probably belonged to the Corieltauvi tribe which had principal centres in Leicester and old Sleaford.

The word 'tribe' can conjure up an image of wild barbarian people, but there is much evidence to show that civilisation had progressed to the extent that the Celtic people were ruled by kings and queens, their spiritual needs were ministered to by priests or druids, and they were traders and skilled craftsmen. It would seem, however, that the main occupation of the settlement at Lincoln was that of fishing, farming and hunting. It is thought that Lincoln's name was originally Lindon, derived from the Celtic word 'llyn' (Celtic for pool). Later it was to be changed by the next inhabitants who were the Romans and who latinised the name to Lindum.

In A.D. 43 the Emperor Claudius invaded Britain and he sent the Ninth Legion Hispania as an advance party, most likely building the roads as they came. Unlike some tribes, the Corieltauvi put up little resistance and during the occupation the tribe lived alongside the Romans, gradually assuming Roman ways and customs. The Romans made Lincoln their most northerly fortress before advancing further and it is thought that they may have built their first fortress downhill, close to the water's edge. By about A.D. 60, however, the fortress had spread over the hillside in the shape of a playing card. In A.D. 71-78 the Ninth Legion moved north to York and for a short period the Second Legion Adiutrix moved in. In A.D. 90 Lindum was created a colonia,

ix

which explains its eventual name 'Lincoln'. Its importance is not to be underestimated; there were only four colonia established in Britain—York, Colchester, Gloucester and Lincoln. It was the highest rank of town to be established, populated mainly by full Roman citizens. The forum was built on top of the hill in the Bailgate area and there was a major programme of building in stone, which was cut from the Greetwell quarries. There is evidence of temples, baths, the forum and probably a theatre. There was a sophisticated water supply and sewers were laid under the streets. Water was taken up from the springs known as the Roaring Meg to the top of the hill, rising as much as 20 metres. The population of Lincoln during the Roman period has been estimated at between five and ten thousand people. At some stage the walls of the city were extended down to the water's edge, which in Roman times came up to the Stonebow. The first gateway on the site of the present Stonebow was built sometime before 211 and was the main gate into the city. There were further fine gates at East gate, West gate, and the North gate, part of which remains as Newport Arch. Lincoln became the centre for the collection of taxes and it became necessary to strengthen the walls for protection. Britain was divided into four provinces and in about 296 Lincoln became the capital of a province called 'Flavia Caesariensis'. There is evidence of a commercial suburb south of the river, where remains of ironworks, pottery kilns, leather shoes, writing implements and butchers' dumps have been found. The river trade became very busy and the Romans were able to move goods from Lincoln to York and on to the coast after building the Fossdyke. Luxuries such as wine, fish-sauce, amphorae of oil, fruits, marble, glass and pottery were imported into Lincoln, making it a sophisticated, cosmopolitan place in which to live.

Archaeologists have found evidence of herbs, corn, barley and hay meadow plants from those times. Religion appeared to be a mixture of the worship of Roman gods such as Augustus, Mercury, Jupiter and Mars and Celtic gods. After Constantine's decision to uphold Christianity there were many Christian converts. Lincoln became a Bishopric from 314, sending a delegate, Bishop Adelfius, to the first Christian Council held in Arles in Southern Gaul in the following year. There is evidence of an early Christian church built on the site of the Roman forum, which has caused much speculation and which probably dates from the late fourth century.

The Roman occupation came to an end in the first half of the fifth century—it is perhaps difficult to appreciate that they were inhabitants for over four hundred years. The next invaders were to be fierce raiders from the present Netherlands, North Germany and Denmark. The former Roman colonia of Lindum became the capital of a small kingdom called Lindsey, 'ey' meaning island, as it was bounded by the rivers Humber, Witham, Trent and the sea. During the late fourth and fifth centuries the former town became blanketed with a layer of 'dark earth' which was common in many late Roman towns. This might well indicate a small self sufficient community mainly concerned with agriculture, horticulture and the keeping of animals. Timber structures began to appear in place of the previous fine stone Roman buildings and evidence has been found of Anglo-Saxon silk, cloth, wood, bone and leather artifacts including shoes. In 628 Bede referred to Blecca, the Praefectus of the city, which could indicate some survival of Roman civic office, but it seems more likely that he was an official of the Northumbrian high king.

By 700 an extraordinary church was built in the forum area, in the form of a basilica like those in Rome. When the remains of the chapel was excavated an important grave was found; the human remains had disappeared but a bronze hanging bowl had been left in position. The bowl is finely decorated with contemporary Celtic craftsmanship and can be seen in the cathedral treasury. By the eighth century new lanes cutting diagonally over the Roman grid and linking the former Roman gates appeared, including Chapel Lane in the upper city and Silver Street in the lower.

During the late ninth century Vikings began to raid Lincoln and caused much havoc, eventually settling before the end of the century. A garrison was established in Lincoln and the town became one of the largest of the 'Five Boroughs' created by the Danes which included Derby, Nottingham, Leicester and Stamford. Not all the inhabitants of the town had Scandinavian names, however, as the names of the moneyers of the Lincoln mint include as many English names as Danish. It is thought that during this period the Wigford suburb developed. The church towers of St Mary le Wigford, St Botolph's and St Peter at Gowts show evidence of Saxon origins, but each tower is not bonded to the church itself which is indicative of earlier churches. The mint was a major producer of coins from at least the mid-10th century, and vied in importance with York after London. The Danes established 12 law men of Lincoln; these may have been the forerunners of the 12 aldermen who were appointed in medieval times. The present street pattern was highly influenced by the Vikings—the Danes laid down Flaxengate (Haralstigh) and Grantham Street (Brancegate). They used copper, silver and possibly amber in their small-scale industries, making rings, beads, textiles, pottery and other artifacts. Lincoln began to thrive again under the Vikings and became a market for the surrounding area. In the 10th century a new waterfront was being constructed on the north side of the river designed for small craft. People trapped and farmed fish on the east side of Brayford Pool. It is thought that the Sincil Dyke might have been cut at this time to help drainage.

By the time the Normans invaded they found a flourishing community. Much of the town was built up and the street system largely in place by 1066. William of Normandy built both the castle and the cathedral church. He established garrisons to protect Lincoln from further local uprisings or invasions of Danes; many families in Lincolnshire had intermarried with the Danes by that time. He built the castle in 1068, demolishing over one hundred houses to make way for it. This brought the feudal system forcibly to Lincoln. The cathedral church was also built with huge defences and the Saxon Bishop of Dorchester, Wulfwig was also the Bishop of Lincoln, assigning 20 out of 60 of his knights to defend the castle. When Wulfwig died William took the opportunity to appoint Remigius, who was a follower and supporter, as bishop and he was responsible for the building of the cathedral, based on Norman designs. Remigius died, however, in 1092, on the day before the new cathedral was to have been consecrated. There were several attempts to seize the castle, the first being in 1138. King Stephen, grandson of William I, tried to retrieve it on one occasion and eventually fought in its defence but was taken prisoner during the Joust of Lincoln. From 1188 Nicholaa de la Haye, a notable Lincoln woman, became Constable and managed to defend it until being relieved by the royal army in a battle that came to be known as the Fair of Lincoln. William the Marshal, the commander in chief of the royal army of King John, forced his way with his army through the West gate of the city and Newport Arch. There was a confused fight in the streets of Lincoln and the rebel barons fled, but were held up at the Great Bargate. It is reputed that 400 knights and barons with their servants were taken prisoners, and that the citizens of Lincoln fled, taking to the river, loaded up with such valuables as they could carry. They eventually returned, when it was safe to do so and there was great rejoicing in Lincoln after the event.

The cathedral has been damaged several times; it was split from top to bottom in a reputed earthquake in 1185. The cathedral was rebuilt by Hugo, son of William, lord of the castle of Avalon, who became known as St Hugh of Lincoln. Hugh appointed Geoffrey de Noiers to reconstruct the cathedral after the earthquake and the pointed Gothic arches were amongst the first to be seen in England. Hugh founded St Mary's Guild whose members undertook to contribute 1,000 marks a year to the fabric fund when the nave was rebuilt. There are many stories of Hugh, who became a beloved character in Lincoln, eventually being canonised. He supervised and reformed the diocese and rebuilt churches that had been allowed to fall into decay. He hated superstition and actively disapproved of relic worship that was prevalent at the time. He loved children and legend has it that a swan at Stow followed him whenever he went to his manor there. St Hugh was succeeded by Bishop Robert Grosseteste, Chancellor of the University of Oxford, and a great scholar. He, in contrast to Hugh, was a fierce disciplinarian who enforced Catholic orthodoxy, and was not popular with the populace. He was strict with the ordinary people; it is said that he ordered his clergy to put a stop to dancing and merrymaking at holiday times in the villages. He had the cathedral enlarged in 1255, and in 1301 the Angel Choir was completed under Bishop Jon de Dalderby and by 1311 the tallest central tower in England had its bells.

In 1194 the citizens of Lincoln bought a charter from Richard I which gave the freedom to trade in any market town without paying toll and lastage. In 1200 the freemen secured a further charter from John giving the right to elect four coroners and two bailiffs as provosts. This freed them from outside interference. The record of a mayor as chief citizen was first heard of in 1206. This brought a common purse and seal. At this time Lincoln became a prosperous city once more through its trade in wool and woollen cloth and there were as many as two hundred spinners in the city. The cloth became famous, especially the fine dyed 'scarlet' and also woollen cloth in off-white, grey and green, which was purchased by the king. Two of the city's woolmen were among the country's most rich and famous attending the great fairs of St Ives and Boston, where wool was sold to Flanders. Guilds and common trades emerged such as potters, barbers, masons, tilers, and weavers. Travellers, however, had to take care as bands of thieves terrorised the highway between Newark and Lincoln. Goods went by water along the Fossdyke to the Trent at Torksey. In 1326 Lincoln became one of the 14 staple towns which meant that all wool, hides, skin, tin and timber being sold in Lincolnshire had to pass through customs in Lincoln before being exported. The staple was inside the walls of the city near the Thornbridge on the Witham. In 1369 it lost its staple; cloth manufacture was shifted to water-powered fulling mills elsewhere and the industry declined.

During the Norman period religion had a powerful influence in the city. Hill gives the highest number of churches in medieval times as 46 and the least 35. Many had been established under pre-Conquest law by thegns or well-to-do burgesses. They were endowed with land called 'the glebe' and received an income in kind by tithes. By the 12th century the Bishop of Lincoln acquired the right to take over the privileges of the churches in the city. Following St Hugh's death, many pilgrims visited his shrine in Lincoln. Diseases now extinct in the west were commonplace at that time and the Sanatorium or Hospital of the Holy Innocents for Lepers, known as the Malandry, stood on land on the edge of the South Common, and the hospice of St Giles gave lodgings for elderly clergy. Many religious orders were established in Lincoln including the Greyfriars, St Catherine's Priory and the Blackfriars. Alongside the religious community of the established church existed a large community of Jewish citizens. The Jews were set apart by the Council of the Church by their dress and were banned from public office; thus they had no authority over Christians. Under Henry I the Jews and their possessions were the property of the king and the king's subjects were expected to protect them. In Lincoln many Jews lived near the castle for protection. The church did not allow Christians to charge interest on loans but Jews, however, could do so and consequently some of them became very wealthy. The king was in severe financial difficulties and turned to Aaron of Lincoln to lend him a considerable fortune. The dean and chapter, together with other landowners, also borrowed money from this wealthy Jew and many found themselves unable to repay their debts. When Aaron died, however, the king took over his fortune.

In 1349 the Black Death hit Lincoln badly and 60 per cent of the clergy died. There was little help for the sick and the dying and by 1360 the city was decaying and its walls were crumbling. Lincoln must have been a sad place at that time. In 1409 the city of Lincoln was created a county and allowed to elect two sheriffs in place of the bailiffs. Tax relief had to be allowed for several years. By 1428 four city parishes had no inhabitants, whilst 17 had under ten persons in them. Houses and churches were falling into ruins and this period was followed by a new dark age.

In 1509, the year Henry VIII became king, Thomas Wolsey was made dean of Lincoln, later to become bishop, and then a cardinal. When he was made Lord Chancellor of England, the city saw him as their patron. He disagreed with the king over his divorce from Catherine of Aragon and fell from grace and it would appear that the citizens of Lincoln mainly supported the king. Henry was declared the supreme head of the church of England at the Stonebow and St Mary of Wigford and all references to Rome were taken out of the church service books. The royal commissioners began dissolving the smaller monasteries in 1535 and there was a 'Rising' amongst the peoples of the Wolds: approximately 2,500 converging on the city to protest against the king. The rebels sent a message to the king, which amongst other demands asked him to change his advisers. The king's very provocative reply was read out in the chapter house of the cathedral:

> I have never read, heard, nor known that Prince's Counsellors and Prelates should be appoynted by rude and ignorant people; nor that they were persons mete or of ability, to disern and choose mete and sufficient counsellors for a Prince. How presumptious then are ye, the rude commons of one shire and that one of the most brute and beastly of the whole realm and of least experience, to find fault with your Prince for the electing of his Counsellors and Prelates.

Although some of the message was omitted, the people were suspicious and withdrew, threatening to go back the next day and attack the gentry. However, the next day the king sent a further proclamation telling the rebels 'to go home ...', and threatening to 'execute all extremity against you, your wives and children without mercy' if they continued one whole day longer in rebellion. The next day all was quiet and the rebellion had been put down. The next year, however, the leaders were tried and hanged, beheaded, drawn and quartered.

The Reformation had an immense effect on the religious houses of Lincoln. St Catherine's was closed in 1538; the friaries in 1539 and finally the cell known as Monks' Abbey. The king sent men to plunder the shrines and take for himself the treasures of the cathedral. By 1549 only nine churches remained out of 38 and the stone from empty churches was used to repair the walls of Brayford Pool. During the Reformation the traditional use of the cathedral was suppressed, and also the cycle of mystery plays—as Beckwith says, 'much of the pageantry had gone out of life.' The Elizabethan years in Lincoln were hard. People suffered from poverty and plagues. The price of basic foodstuffs such as beans, oats, barley and rye had risen and the populace could not afford them. The government introduced a series of measures to deal with the poor, labelling those who were able-bodied but very poor as the sturdy beggars. The Elizabethan Poor Law was set up from a rate collected on a parish basis; newcomers to Lincoln were expelled by the 'master of the poor'.

In 1596 a room under the Greyfriars building became a jersey knitting and spinning shop to set poor children to work. The poor became dependent on private charity and endowments. There were at least three outbreaks of plague in the 16th century; because of the sickness there was an influx of beggars and St Lawrence's Church became known as the 'pest' church. Hiring fairs were set up at the Stonebow and servants and workmen had to attend to hire themselves for a year to a master. If you were considered one of the lower orders at this time then life would have been very hard. Conditions in the city got even worse during the Civil War of the 17th century, though when Charles I visited Lincoln in 1642 he was given a rapturous welcome. Control of the city, however, swung first to one side then the other.

A royalist garrison occupied Lincoln but surrendered to the Earl of Manchester in October 1643. Although Lincoln was occupied by a crack Parliamentary regiment it again went to the royalists. Finally in 1644 the Earl of Manchester reoccupied the lower city and routed the royalist defences of the castle. 650 men were taken prisoner and many houses sacked. Churches and the Bishop's Palace were destroyed and the Eleanor Cross was smashed. When the monarchy was restored in 1661, seven aldermen, other officers and the town clerk were stripped of their office for having supported Parliament. The result of the ravages of the Reformation and the Civil War were noted by Daniel Defoe who described Lincoln in 1712 as 'an ancient, ragged and still decaying city, it is so full of the ruins of monasteries and religious houses, that in short, the very barns, stables, outhouses ... were built church fashion; that is to say with stone walls and arched windows and door'.

During the 18th century, Lincoln's fortunes began to change again. The *Lincoln Gazette*; the *Lincoln Journal* and the *Lincoln, Rutland and Stamford Mercury* began publication. The first theatre was established in 1744 near the Harlequin on Castle Hill, moving to the High Street later. The Theatre Royal was built in 1806 but burnt down in 1892; it reopened as the present theatre in 1893. The Assembly Rooms were built in 1744 on the Bail and stuff balls were held there under the patronage of Lady Banks, wife of Sir Joseph Banks. Downhill, the city Assembly Rooms opened over the Butter Market. The races had started on Lincoln Heath, south of the city, in 1597 but after enclosure they moved, first to Welton, then to the Carholme.

By 1780 the nonconformists began making an impact in Lincoln. The Methodist Society started from a lumber room near Gowt's Bridge, then moved to Waterside South and in turn to an elegant building in Clasketgate. The Society of Friends had established their Meeting House in Beaumont Fee in 1685 and the Free Methodists, Baptists and Presbyterians followed.

By 1780 the problem of the poor became apparent and 13 city parishes, under the provisions of Gilbert's Act, got together to set up a House of Industry. Women spun hemp and men broke stones for roads and farms. Children were apprenticed to frame-work knitters. These were no doubt harsh measures but reflected current thinking. The first hospital for the city and county was established in 1765 with ten beds in a former maltings on Waterside South. In 1777 a purpose-built hospital was established, later occupied by the Theological College. The Lawn mental institution was set up in 1820 in a fine building with an ornamental columned portico in seven acres of grounds. Dr. Francis Willis began to specialise in mental illness and his advice was widely sought after treating King George III. His innovative work was continued by Dr. Charlesworth who strove to bring about the end of mechanical restraint and straitjackets.

John Howard the prison reformer was highly critical of the city gaol in the Stonebow when he visited in 1784, describing it as 'the worst in the country'. He found criminals locked in dungeons with earth floors. In 1809 a new city prison and court house was completed on the site of the Sessions House on Lindum Hill. The Reform Act of 1832 did away with the 45-man self-appointed corporation and replaced this with a town council of 25 elected by some of the citizens. By 1839 a Union Workhouse was opened on a site alongside the House of Industry near the Lawn Hospital. Those judged to be paupers were forced to live in it; men on one side, women on the other. Lincoln began to achieve prosperity again by the mid-1800s. Many new houses were built and local brickyards struggled to produce enough bricks. The population more than doubled between 1801 and 1851. The area round Sincil Street developed in the 1840s with new residents coming from the countryside.

There were over eighty projected railway schemes for Lincoln. Two companies, the Great Northern and the Midland built two stations; the Midland station in St Mark's parish was completed by 1846 in classical architecture and the second station, the Central, was opened in 1848, resulting in two crossings in the High Street. The tracks and sidings occupied a large area of Lincoln and the railway companies became property owners.

Times were still hard for the general populace in the mid-19th century and the infant mortality rate in Lincoln was three times the national average. In 1856 a cemetery was opened on the South Common followed 40 years later by others on Washingborough Road and on Newport. In 1826 the Lincoln dispensary was established on the Cornhill for poor people. In 1907 it moved to Silver Street, then to Mint Street where later it became the Chest Clinic. In 1878 the new County Hospital was opened on the edge of the city, replacing the hundred-year-old building near the castle. Mrs. Annie Bromhead had established an Institute of Nursing on Greestone Terrace. Her nurses were used in the typhoid fever epidemic in 1904. Because of the large numbers of victims in the epidemic, 1,045 cases and 131 deaths, the County Hospital could not cope and the drill hall and other parish halls were equipped as makeshift hospitals. The city's water supply was found to be contaminated and after much prevarication by the council a new water supply was brought from Elkesley, in Nottinghamshire, in 1911.

The 19th century brought tremendous growth to Lincoln due to the establishment of industry. In 1842 Clayton and Shuttleworth began making steam engines, eventually employing over 1,400 men. Charles Duckering began making stoves, machinery and sanitary ironwork and in 1851 William Foster started to produce threshing machines.

Robert Robey exhibited his iron-framed threshing machines in the Royal Show held in Lincoln in 1907. In 1857 Joseph Ruston established Ruston Proctor and Company which eventually gave employment to over 1,600 people, and in 1875 Robey's were producing many engines, including a winding engine for the Duke of Sutherland's coal pits. Robey's and Ruston's took the highest awards at the European Industrial Exhibition and their engines could be seen working in many countries including Australia and Russia.

In 1828 the Lincoln Gas-Light and Coke Company was formed and the city was the second place in the country to have gas lamps. The original site of the gas works was near Brayford on the Carholme Road, and when this became too small a new gas works was built at Bracebridge. Electricity came later; in 1898 a generating station was erected at Brayford Waterside North, although some of the larger companies had been generating their own electricity before this date. The Lincoln Co-operative Society was set up in 1861 due to the inspiration of Mr. Thomas Parker who became its secretary. The Co-operative Society was very active and a mill, engine house, bakery and warehouse were set up on Waterside North. They also set up a slaughter house, hide and skin market on Sincil Bank. The Co-operative Society also erected workers' housing, formed women's groups, an education committee, and provided a library and newsroom free of charge. Towards the end of the 19th century there was evidence of much poverty in the city, despite the growth of industry. In the 1870s soup kitchens were a regular feature of everyday life and halfpenny dinners were provided for children. In 1890 Joseph Ruston built the Drill Hall for the Volunteers and provided it with appliances for cooking in large quantities for large numbers. In 1893 a series of 'Robin dinners' were given to 1,200 children at Christmas. With poverty came drunkenness—in 1869 there were 183 public houses in Lincoln. The temperance movement attempted to re-educate people into sobriety and two large temperance halls were built in Lincoln. There were temperance processions and concerts to promote the drinking of healthy water. This was ironic when Lincoln was in great difficulties over the supply of clean water to its citizens.

Education in Lincoln was greatly expanded during the 19th century and became available for girls as well as boys. The National School was founded in 1812 as part of the movement controlled by the Church of England. The first infant school was established in Langworthgate in 1829 and the Victoria Infants' School at St Peter at Gowts was built to celebrate the queen's coronation in 1838. This was followed by the Wesleyan Day School in Grantham Street and the British School in Newland and Diocesan Training School in Newport. The Bluecoat School was in Michael's Mount. There were 15 public schools by the mid-1800s including the long-established grammar school and Christ's Hospital School, and 42 private schools. New schools were opened in Rosemary Lane in 1860 for 600 children. The School for Science and Art was started in the Corn Exchange in 1863, moving first to Silver Street and later to the north side of Monks Road. This building then housed the City School and later became part of the Art College. Night classes were started for working men, taught by students of the theological college. The first school built by the City Council was Monks Road School for infants and juniors. A Mechanics' Institute was housed in the Greyfriars building, later moving to the Assembly Rooms over the butter market. The Workers' Education Association was established in 1911 in the Co-operative Education Rooms, later moving to Danesgate, then to the building on Beaumont Fee, providing education for many adults in the city. As people learned to read there was a demand for libraries and the new permanent library was formed in 1822, holding 5,000 books. The YMCA formed a library in Guildhall Street and the City of Lincoln Public Library was established in the Assembly Rooms over the butter market in Silver Street.

In the mid- to late 19th century many of the medieval parish churches were restored or enlarged and several new churches and chapels were built, including St Hugh's Catholic Church (1893) and St Nicolas, Newport (1840). A new housing estate was created in St Giles parish in the 1930s and St Peter at Arches Church, which used to stand opposite the present Binns Store, was moved there in 1936. Transport began to improve when horse-drawn trams were introduced along the High Street in 1882. In 1905 the company was acquired by Lincoln Corporation and electric trams began to run. Motor buses took over after 1929.

During the First World War Lincoln firms were diverted to aircraft and munitions manufacture. Women were encouraged to go into the works, welding, fitting and operating complex machinery. Lincoln became one of the major production centres of aircraft during the war. Ruston's built over 2,000 planes, including the famous Sopwith Camels. Robey's built many aircraft including the Sopwith Gunbus, the Short 184 Seaplane, Longhorns, and the Robey Peters Fighting Machine. Clayton and Shuttleworth produced Sopwith Triplanes and Camels, and the Handley Page Bomber in the great Titanic Works. The planes were tested on the West Common. Fosters were commissioned to develop the first British tank. During the Second World War the factories turned again to the production of munitions and once more women were employed. Lincoln suffered some bomb damage in the Monks Road and lower High Street areas and urban fringes.

Lincoln has had a lively entertainment history; the Palace Theatre was opened in 1871 in the Masonic Hall in Newland. This building became the Empire Music Hall and then the Plaza Cinema until being hit by an incendiary bomb in 1943. Cinemas have included the Cinematograph on the Cornhill; the Grand Electric Cinema on the High Street; Central Cinema, St Swithins's Square; The Regal, High Street; the Savoy on Saltergate; the Odeon on the High Street and the Radion on Newport; now the home of Radio Lincolnshire. The Lincoln City Football team has been much in evidence, starting in 1861 and being reformed in 1883. 'Trip week', the week before the August bank holiday week, began in the 1870s and gave great numbers of people the opportunity to visit the coastal towns of Skegness and Cleethorpes.

During the early 20th century Lincoln expanded, creating new housing estates, including Swanpool and St Giles, based on the idea of garden suburbs. Later came the Ermine Estate and Birchwood. In 1974 the High Street was pedestrianised for easier shopping.

Politically, Lincoln has changed its alliances between the major parties. Arthur Taylor was the first Labour member of Parliament in 1924. George Deer defeated Sir Walter Luddell to become Labour MP in 1945. In 1973 the city's member of Parliament, Dick Taverne, founded the Democratic Labour Party which took control of the City Council. Margaret Jackson took the seat in 1974, losing to Kenneth Carlisle who held it from 1979 to 1997. Gillian Merrion, Labour, took the seat in May 1997.

In the 1960s and '70s there were major building programmes in Lincoln including the Pelham Bridge Flyover, the new telephone exchange, Co-op House, the *Eastgate Hotel*, and Wigford Way. Some old friends were lost, such as the swing bridge over the

Brayford and some relics of Lincoln's industrial heritage alongside the Brayford. The Christmas Market, based on the market at Neustadt, Lincoln's twin town in Germany, has grown to be extremely popular, attracting visitors from all over the world.

Our story begins and finishes, however, with the Brayford Pool. The first dwellers lived by the pool in the Iron Age. In 1996 the new university building rose on the banks of the Brayford. The new bridge which connects Tritton Road to the Carholme Road has opened up further vistas of the magnificent cathedral standing high on the hill which was once occupied by the Roman forum. Visually Lincoln remains one of the most inspiring European cities, full of historical interest.

1 Our story starts and finishes with Brayford Pool. Evidence shows that the earliest settlers in Lincoln were from a tribe known as the 'Corieltauvi' whose principal centres are believed to have been in Leicester and Old Sleaford. The Iron-Age culture which appeared *c*.500 B.C. was richly developed; traces of a round hut and pottery fragments have been found by Brayford Pool. The first syllable of 'Lin' could be attributed to the Welsh word 'llyn', a lake.

2 This is the view of Lincoln that we get as we approach it from the Carholme Road. The windmill, water tower and the cathedral are familiar landmarks on the skyline. The cliff-edge of limestone above the West Common shows the ancient Jurassic routeway. During the Ice Age, glacial action forced a gap about a mile wide, forming a huge river. The flat land on either side of the Carholme would have been covered in water. Brayford Pool was formed by the meeting of the Rivers Witham and Till.

3 It is remarkable that 19 boats such as this one have been found in the Witham from the earliest settlement. This one was found at Fiskerton and belongs to the City and County Museum. Its use reinforces the importance of the river for transportation and early trading.

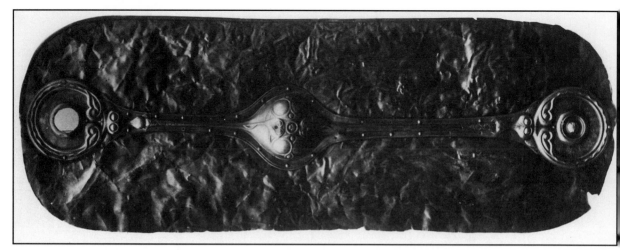

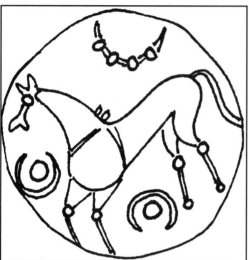

4 *Above*. This is the famous Witham shield, found in the river in 1826 and now in the British Museum. It would be wrong to think of the Corieltauvi tribe as being wild and unskilled; the work on the shield indicates quite the opposite. It is decorated with a wild boar design with coral. Photographs do not do it justice and a visit to the British Museum should be made.

5 *Left*. This Corieltauvi coin with a lively horse design, which was often repeated, was found at South Ferriby. The mint is believed to have been at Sleaford where clay moulds to cast pellets of gold or silver have been found. The design on the reverse of the coin was often a boar echoing the design on the Witham shield.

6 *Below*. In A.D. 43 Emperor Claudius invaded Britain, sending the Ninth Legion Hispania as an advance party, most likely building the roads as they came. Ermine Street and Tillbridge Lane are early roads from this period. They called their settlement 'Lindum' and, if they did experience any resistance from the Iron-Age people, this was soon quashed and the two communities lived alongside each other. The Romans were to live in Lincoln for the next four hundred years.

7 There is some speculation as to whether there was an earlier fortress close to the water's edge but this reconstruction shows the uphill fortress which is believed to have dated from A.D. 54-65. The fortress contained a basilica, chapel and regimental offices in timber. We can see how the Ermine Street cuts through the fortress; eventually to become the Fosseway. By about A.D. 60 the fortress spread over the hillside in the shape of a playing card which forms the basis of the present street pattern.

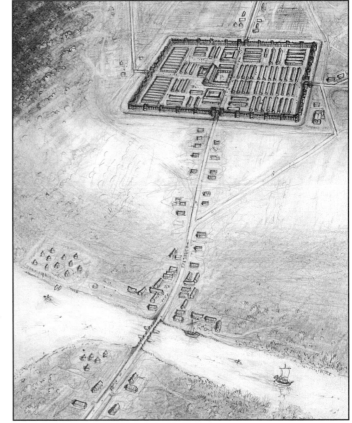

8 Sometime before A.D. 96 the Romans made Lindum into a colonia, hence its eventual name of Lincoln. This was the highest rank of town created, populated by full Roman citizens. The second *forum-basilica* was built on top of the old one looking eastwards. Stone was now used for the principal buildings and porticoed walkways overlooked the central piazza. A magnificent colonnade provided an elegant frontage onto the present Bailgate.

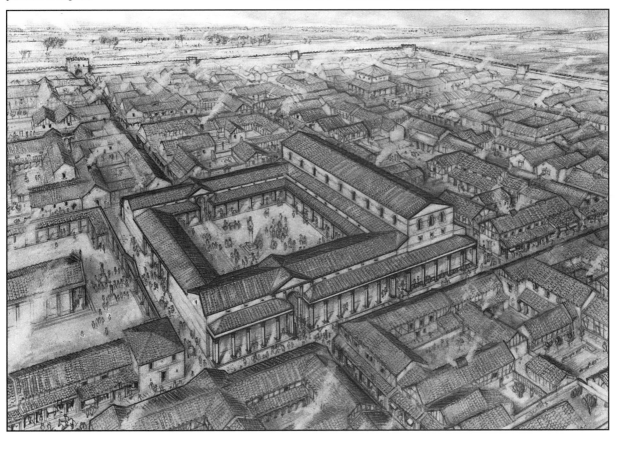

9 A photograph by Marris, taken in the 1900s in Bailgate, shows a scene that is not so different from that of today, apart from the costumes of the girls, boys and adults. Instead of cars lining the road there are horse-drawn carriages and bicycles. On the road we can just see the remains of the base of Roman columns which formed part of the forum. These are more easily seen today. More substantial remains are to be found in the basements of several of the houses on the Bail.

10 This photograph was taken in the late 19th century and shows workmen uncovering part of the colonnade of the *forum-basilica*. Since the Romans were in Lincoln the road level has risen a great deal.

11 This early photograph of the 1860s shows the fair as it stood on Orchard Street on the site of the present DSS building. If we look up the hill towards the castle we can see the line of the Roman city wall which went down to the river; traces of the wall can still be seen on Motherby Hill today.

12 This artist's impression gives us an idea of Roman building methods which were used for temples and baths and fine villas. The picture illustrates the building of the Stonebow Centre. A postern gate for pedestrians was built in the fourth century, the base of which can be seen beneath the Royal Bank of Scotland.

13 The Roman postern gateway showing the flagged surface of the entrance.

14 All over Lincoln traces have been found of Roman gateways, arches and walls. It is remarkable that Newport arch still stands and is driven under every day. This photograph of the early 1900s shows the arch standing beside the house which is still there. The shop on the left-hand side once belonged to Lincoln Co-operative Society and traces of its name can still be seen on the side of the building which is now a Chinese restaurant. The shop on the right-hand side of the picture has gone and has made way for the Bailgate Methodist Church.

15 It is now good to see that the West gate of the castle, close to the West gate of the Roman city has been restored and forms another entrance to the castle from Union Road. The castle originally contained a Shire Hall, where the sheriff held his court, and the living quarters of the constable. Until the 1830s the castle was legally part of the county and outside the jurisdiction of the City Council. Visitors to the castle can see a copy of the Magna Carta, sent to Lincoln in 1215. Although the document talked of freedom and liberty for the citizen, the feudal system bound society together in a series of hierarchical relationships, with the king at the top and the landless peasants at the bottom.

16 This hanging bowl made of bronze is one of Lincoln's most exciting finds and has caused much speculation. It has celtic designs and has been dated somewhere between the fourth and seventh centuries. It was found in a grave on the site of a very early church which predates that of St Paul in the Bail. The body had gone but the bowl remained and, whilst it indicates an early Christian community, this type of bowl could be associated with pagan burials.

17 *Above left*. Lincoln's next invaders were to be the Angles and the Saxons and this old postcard shows evidence of Saxon building. Only the tower of St Mary le Wigford is of the late Saxon period; likewise the towers of St Peter at Gowt's and St Botolph's ranged along the High Street. The towers are not bonded to the churches, indicating that they are churches from an earlier period. Standing in front of the church is a stone conduit, which was made from the stone taken from the Carmelite Friary in 1539. This conduit was part of the medieval water supply and used as a source of water over many centuries.

18 *Above right*. This is an intriguing dedication stone built into St Mary le Wigford Church. The dedication reads from the bottom and translated says: 'Eirtig had me built and endowed to the glory of Christ and St Mary.' Eirtig was a Danish name and introduces us to Lincoln's next invaders, the Vikings. It is interesting that Eirtig used the top of a Roman tombstone to carve his dedication. The tombstones seemed to have been in plentiful supply after the Roman occupation.

19 *Opposite, above*. This is an artist's impression of the waterfront at Brayford in the 11th century, during the late Viking period. The Vikings created smaller industries of textiles, pottery and other artifacts in the Flaxengate area and Lincoln became a market for the surrounding area. A new waterfront was constructed and people trapped and farmed fish on the east side of Brayford Pool.

20 *Opposite, below*. In the 11th century the Normans reached Lincoln and this aerial view shows clearly the layout of the castle built by William the Conqueror in 1068. William built it for a defence since the Vikings were still hostile and by this time many Lincolnshire people were of Viking descent. The Victorian prison building and the Court House were later additions. The substantial ditch was not intended to hold water and became occupied by market traders. Many hangings took place from the gallows, hence the name of the public house on Westgate, *The Strugglers*. The gallows used to stand across the road at the junction with Burton Road.

21 Greestone steps originates from the Danish name of Greenstone Stephs. They are to be found on Lindum Hill and climb up to the cathedral alongside the De Montford University building which was once Christ's Hospital School for Girls and later the Art College.

22 This tower, now known as the observatory, was built as a result of a treaty between King Stephen and the powerful Ranulph, Earl of Chester during the uprising that became known as 'the anarchy'. The little observatory tower was added in the 19th century to indulge a prison governor's interest in astronomy and was used during the Second World War to send and receive signals from Nottingham Castle.

23 An aerial picture of the present cathedral taken in 1996 showing the close houses standing around it. It has recently been cleaned and restored and has a constant stream of visitors. John Ruskin described it as 'out and out the most precious piece of architecture in the British Isles, and roughly speaking, worthy of any two other Cathedrals we have'. William Cobbett, writing in 1830, called it simply 'the finest building in the whole world'.

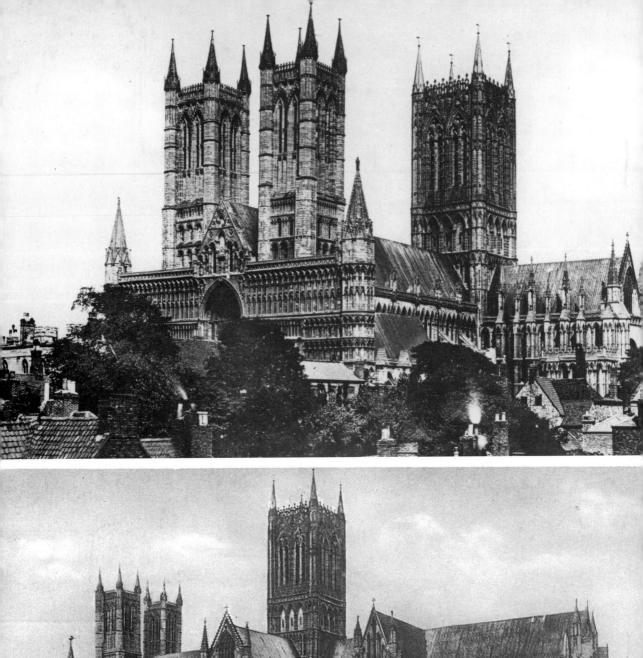

24 *Left.* This postcard, taken earlier this century, shows the west front of the present cathedral, which was the original Norman front of the building. The first cathedral was built by Remigius and was consecrated in 1092, the day after he died. The building was almost completely destroyed by a reputed earthquake in 1186 and the present building, designed by Hugh of Avalon, was started in 1192. The cathedral walls are massive as it was built as part of the defences of the city.

25 *Below left.* This unusual view of the cathedral was taken from the south east, perhaps from the top of the then new Christ's Hospital Girl's School, which later became the Art College. It shows the Tithe Barn in the right foreground and the back of Vicars' Court on the left.

26 *Below.* A view of the south porch. On the end of this portion of the building are the statues of Edward I and Queen Eleanor, who died at Harby. The remains of the Eleanor Cross, which was erected at the base of Cross O'Cliff Hill, are to be found in the grounds of the castle.

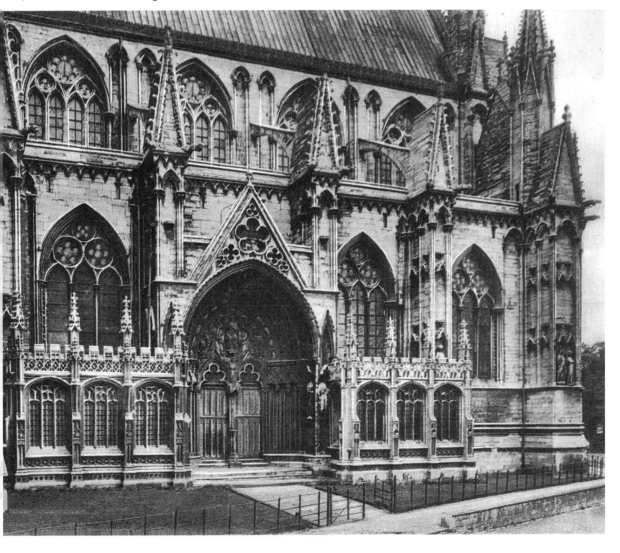

27 *Above*. This engraving was completed in 1743 by Samuel and Nathaniel Buck and shows the cathedral as it looked with two steeples, although it had three when it was rebuilt. The large steeple on the tower fell down sometime in the 1500s. The other two spires were eventually taken down in 1808. The first attempt, in 1726, was frustrated by a large mob of people.

28 *Left*. Potter Gate is the gate at the eastern end of the cathedral close and was locked at night. This photograph of 1928 shows a very peaceful scene, and the arch before the walls were removed on each side to make way for traffic.

29 *Right*. The Exchequer gate is one of the medieval gates to the cathedral close. It dates from the reign of Edward I and has been much restored. It was built to house the dean and chapter's financial records, including the registers of their many estates. The gates of the close were also locked at curfew until well into the 18th century.

30 An engraving by T. Waghorn showing the cathedral from Brayford wharf, 1914.

31 Following the earthquake in 1185 Hugh of Avalon, who was eventually canonised for his piety and strength of character, rebuilt the cathedral in the French style. The pointed arches were amongst the first to be seen in England. The east end or choir was the first to be built and it was not until well into the 13th century that work began on the nave.

32 *Above left.* This rare marble font is to be seen at the west end of the cathedral. It has pre-Christian symbols and is an example of Tournai work from Flanders, dated 1145, which probably belonged to the earlier Norman cathedral.

33 *Above right.* The cathedral is a delight to all visitors, as there are many stone carvings to be found all over the building. These are small medieval figures.

34 *Below left.* One of the most famous of these stone carvings is the Lincoln Imp, which visitors love to find. He sits up on top of a pillar at the east end of the cathedral. The legend of the Lincoln Imp has become famous all over the world, promoted by the jeweller Mr. Usher who founded the Usher Gallery collection.

35 *Below right.* The chapter house was the scene of a parliamentary meeting in 1301 whilst King Edward was on the throne. He met in Lincoln so that he could continue with his preparations for war with Scotland. Altogether 300 people met, representing the barons, the church, the law and the universities. It is said that corn and hay were provided for 400 horses for a month, and 300 sheep were eaten. Sixty dozen of good parchments were used by the clerks and 3,121 gallons of ale were drunk at a penny a gallon.

36 & 37 The Tennyson statue is a well loved statue at the north-east end of the cathedral, dedicated to the poet who lived at Somersby in the Wolds. Eight houses were removed to create this very pleasant corner. There is a Tennyson Research Centre in Lincoln Castle. This photograph was taken at the dedication service on 15 July 1905.

38 During medieval times one-tenth of a citizen's income had to be paid to the church for its upkeep. Often the tithe was paid in kind and barns such as this built in 1440 were erected to store the tithes. The barn stands at the top of Greestone Steps and was once the dining room of Christ's Hospital School for Girls. The walls are massive with huge buttresses and it is a very impressive building.

39 & 40 These two boundary bond stones mark the limits of the Norman city jurisdiction and bear the city arms. They can be found the width of a ditch below the line of the Roman south bail gate on Steep Hill and to the north of Newport Arch.

41 The seal of the Malandry. The Malandry, or Hospital of the Holy Innocents, stood on the site of Bernadette House, Residential Home for the elderly, which used to be St Botolph's Vicarage. During the Middle Ages the hospital extended over the triangular field at the base of Cross O'Cliff Hill, close to St Catherine's Priory. Leprosy was regarded as a punishment for sin and lepers were forbidden to enter any church, mill, bakehouse or to address strangers. The leper was given a rattle to warn people of his approach. St Hugh of Avalon, who rebuilt the cathedral, is reputed to have bathed the lepers in his own chamber.

42 St Mary's Guild Hall stands on the present High Street, on the line of Ermine Street on top of Roman remains. A prominent group of merchants founded St Mary's Guild, a socio-religious organisation, in 1251. It met in Wigford in this building, which is reputed to have been built originally for Henry II's residence at the time of his visit in 1157. The merchants supported each other legally and financially, if necessary. This photograph was taken in 1891 by Robert Slingsby, one of Lincoln's first photographers, and shows a group of Lincoln's inhabitants nicely positioned with their perambulators.

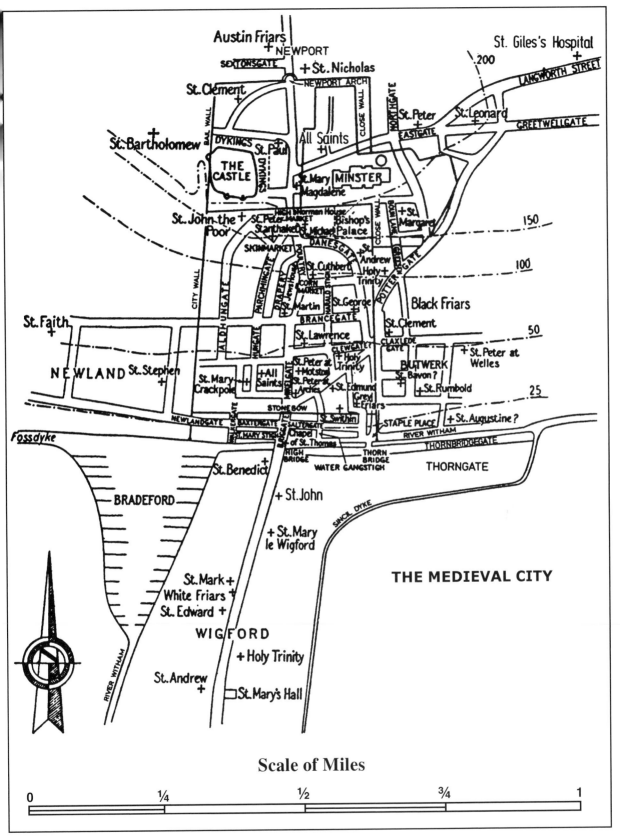

Austin Friars
+ NEWPORT
SEXTONSGATE
St. Clement
+
St. Bartholomew
DYKINGS St. Paul
THE
CASTLE
St. John the
Poor + SC.Peter
STANTHAKEGT
SKINMARKET
St. Nicholas
NEWPORT ARCH
All Saints
+
St. Mary
Magdalene
HIGH NORMAN HOUSE
Bishop's
Michael Palace
DANESGATE
St. Cuthbert
CORN
MARKET
DRAPERY
St. Martin
St. Peter
St. George
BRANCEGATE
St. Lawrence
CLEWGATE
St. Peter at
+ Motstal
St. Peter at
+ Arches
St. Swithin

St. Giles's Hospital
+
200
LANGWORTH STREET
St. Peter
EASTGATE
St. Leonard
GREETWELLGATE
150
St.
Margaret
100
St.
Andrew
Holy
Trinity
Black Friars
St. Clement
CLAXLEDE
GATE
50
BUTWERK
St. Bavon?
St. Peter at
Welles
St. Rumbold
25
Grey
Friars
St. Edmund
STAPLE PLACE
St. Augustine?
RIVER WITHAM
THORNBRIDGEGATE

St. Faith

NEWLAND St. Stephen

CITY WALL
ALDHUNGATE
HUNGATE
St. Mary
Crackpole
+All
Saints
HOLY Trinity

STONEBOW
St. Swithin
NEWLANDGATE
BAXTERGATE
SALTERGATE
St. Mary STREET
Chapel
of St. Thomas
HIGH
BRIDGE
WATER GANGSTICH
THORN
BRIDGE
THORNGATE

Fossdyke

St. Benedict

BRADEFORD

RIVER WITHAM

+ St. John

+ St. Mary
le Wigford

St. Mark +
White Friars +
St. Edward +

WIGFORD

SINCIL DYKE

THE MEDIEVAL CITY

+ Holy Trinity

St. Andrew
+

St. Mary's Hall

Scale of Miles

| 0 | ¼ | ½ | ¾ | 1 |

43 This map of the medieval city shows the vast number of churches that were established and present in medieval times. It appears that the highest number of medieval parish churches in Lincoln at any one time was forty-six.

44 This photograph of Jew's House, taken in the late 19th century, illustrates a beautiful two-storied house built in the late 12th century. The ground-floor front wall had small round-arched openings for shops, later altered to rectangular openings. The hall was on the upper floor. Immediately to the right is Jew's Court. It is believed that Jew's Court was a Jewish synagogue and in 1997 a service of re-dedication took place for the Jewish community, who have returned to their worship after a gap of 700 years. Jew's Court contains a bookshop run by the Lincolnshire Society for History and Archaeology. It is thought that the Jewish community set up its shops and houses close to the castle to receive protection from the king.

45 St Giles Hospital stood on the north side of Wragby Road, opposite Curie Avenue. The hospital was first mentioned in 1280—the vicars of the cathedral being closely connected with it. Weak and infirm vicars were admitted for rest and recuperation. Richard de Ravenser, Archdeacon of Lincoln in the 14th century, ordered that 12 pensioners should be supported in the hospital and given 1s. 2d. daily for food and 4s. yearly for clothes.

46 The High Bridge dates from 1160. On its east side was a chapel of St Thomas of Canterbury, built before 1200, soon after the murder of Thomas Becket. In 1549 the Reformation led to the desecration of the chapel. It was later used by the Guild of Tanners and Butchers as an assembly room and by the middle of the 18th century it was being used as a chandler's shop. It was eventually pulled down in 1763.

The present building on the west side dates from 1601 and is reputed to be Britain's earliest surviving shop on a bridge. At one time fish and meat were sold on it.

47 On the other side of the High Bridge stood an obelisk which was erected when the remains of the chapel dedicated to St Thomas the Martyr were removed in 1763 and the street widened. The obelisk housed a water conduit, the source being the Monks Spring on the hillside above Monks Road. The obelisk was removed in 1939 at the start of the war and kept in storage until 1996 when it was re-erected in the new St Mark's Square shopping precinct. (See Fig. 179).

48 This atmospheric painting of a boat passing under the Glory Hole was painted by Peter de Wint and photographed by Harrison, one of the early photographers. Young women are collecting water from the river which was a common practice at the time and unfortunately led to outbreaks of infectious diseases such as typhoid.

49 There are several very fine 15th-century timber-framed buildings and inns in Lincoln and the *Harlequin* is a much loved landmark on Steep Hill. It is picturesquely positioned on the corner of Michaelgate and half sunk into the road. It is now one of Lincoln's antique bookshops, haunted by collectors.

50 *The Witch and the Wardrobe* stands on Waterside and is a 16th-century building with an early 18th-century front. It is named after C.S. Lewis' children's story and was formerly the A1 fish restaurant. Nearby stands The Green Dragon, formerly a 14th-century wool merchant's house with timber gables added in the 16th century.

51 The Stonebow has been the site of a gateway since the Roman period, and the overhead chamber has been used for council meetings since the 13th century. The present building was begun in the 15th century. There are two 13th-century elongated figures of the Annunciation on the front. Until 1809 the ground floor served as the city gaol. A narrow lane ran alongside and a grated window in the prison wall enabled prisoners to talk to passers-by who fed them with food and drink. The felons were kept in two dungeons with damp earth floors. They had no exercise, no water supply, no straw and, when they were released, they had to pay the gaoler for their keep. A visitor in 1802 said that the prisoners were half starved, half suffocated and in a state of continual intoxication.

52 The Sessions House, a plain brick Georgian building, stands on the corner of Lindum Hill and Monks Road. It was designed by William Hayward and built in 1805. The first sessions were heard in 1809 and the gaol at the back replaced the one in the Stonebow that was so heavily criticised by John Howard the prison reformer. This building housed the Magistrates' Court and the gaol became the old police station until the building known as Ryvita House was built in 1970. The photograph was taken in 1959—the building is presently being adapted by North Lincolnshire College.

53 The Assize Court building which stands in the castle grounds was completed in 1826, the architect being Robert Smirke, who also designed the British Museum. It is of gothic design with castellation and is now the Crown Court building. In the foreground is part of the old prison, built in 1787 by Carr of York and Wm Lumby, which continued in use until 1878. It was innovative for its day as it had an exercise yard for prisoners.

54 Visitors to the old prison chapel are intrigued and sometimes frightened as they try out the Separate System pews. The pews are high sided and as you enter a door shuts you in a separate compartment. There are no seats, just ledges, and prisoners were kept in solitary confinement under the new Pentonville or Separate System designed to keep prisoners away from the bad influence of other felons. The chapel is the only surviving original example where the pews ensured that prisoners could see only the chaplain, not each other. Condemned felons were on the back row, and women on the front row. Debtors were curtained off from the others.

55   Pevsner describes the Judges Lodging which stands in Castle Square as the finest house of its date in Lincoln. It was built in 1810 by William Hayward of smooth cold stock brick. Judges presiding at the Assizes, now the Crown Court, lodge here overnight. There is quite a crowd here on this Edwardian postcard and police stand on duty. It could have been the start of the Assizes, or another important event in Lincoln.

56   The prison on Greetwell Road was built in 1869-72 by Frederick Peck of London, when the old prison in the castle grounds closed. It was built on the open grid system. The front of the building is gothic with a castellated gateway and lodges with romanesque touches. The prison is built of red brick with stone details. Many thousands of prisoners have been housed here and the back buildings are as high as six storeys.

57 This fine new Magistrates Court on the High Street, opposite the new C & A complex, was opened by HRH Prince of Wales on Tuesday, 20 November 1990. It has separate court rooms that are well designed and furnished and has a completely different atmosphere from the old Sessions House. A coffee bar supplies the court officials and visitors with light refreshments.

58 A once familiar sight, as one approached Lincoln along the Carholme, were the mills that stood on the cliff edge. Sadly, not many photographers took pictures probably because the sight was too familiar. One mill that was photographed was Hobbler's Hole mill which was situated close to the roundabout at the top of Yarborough Road and Burton Road. Some of the other mills were known as Ellis's Mill, which was restored and is open to the public, Whitton's Mill, Harrison's Mill and Ward's Mill (demolished in 1920).

59 It is difficult for new-comers to Lincoln to have any idea that there was once a great Union Workhouse close to the Lawn Hospital, built to house 360 people in 1837 under the new Poor Law. The workhouse was designed by N.A. Nicholson and cost £11,000. It followed the normal pattern and was symmetrical, so that families could be split up; men on one side, women on the other. It also housed many children. In the 1860s it became the overnight stop for vagrants and tramps and in 1879 the inmates over-flowed into the militia barracks. It gradually took the form of a hospital and a nurses' home was built at the rear. It was still in use until 1963, then called West View, when it housed the elderly in rather grim surrounds. It was demolished in 1965.

60 This was the last meeting of the Board of Guardians on 25 March 1930, who presided over the Workhouse that stood on Willis Close. If you walk along Burton Road you can see the remains of the entrance to the workhouse close to the corner of Union Street, which is a reminder of part of Lincoln's history which has almost disappeared.

61 This is a postcard of the girls' home situated on Belle View Road and Belle View Terrace, close to the workhouse. Mrs. Danby and others established a Girls' Friendly Society Home for girls living in the workhouse and going into domestic service, to give them training and find places for them. This plan was installed after 1870 when boarding out became the norm for the children in the workhouse. The girls' home later became the Gas House, occupied by the local office of the East Midlands Gas Board. It was demolished in 1979.

62 This postcard could be an interior shot of the Girls' Friendly Society Home with the girls practising their ironing skills. No doubt they would have been kept very busy with all the washing and ironing from the workhouse, and later West View.

53 An early engraving by the architects William Watkins and Joseph Liversey, who designed The Lawn Lunatic Asylum, set up in 1820 in an elegant building in seven acres of grounds. It is associated with Dr. E.P. Charlesworth, who, with Mr. Robert Gardiner-Hill, practised the system called 'non-restraint' which discarded strait-jackets and shackles. Innovative work was done by Dr. Francis Willis who treated King George III. The walls to the grounds were even built below the edge of the hill so that the patients did not feel confined. Now visitors can enjoy a peaceful pint in the solitary confinement cells since The Lawns was successfully transformed to a leisure complex which also houses the archaeology section.

54 King George III is now safely confined in the castle grounds. The bust stands near the Bath House and is made from coadestone, a type of terracotta, and it is just the top of a full-length statue that used to stand on the top of Dunston Pillar, at Dunston Heath. The statue was erected in 1810 to replace a beacon or land lighthouse to guide travellers across the heath. It became a hazard to air traffic during the Second World War and the statue was removed.

65 This is a reconstruction of an early train leaving Central Station on its way towards Gainsborough on the Great Northern line. The two railway crossings on the High Street have infuriated visitors and citizens of Lincoln for many years. The first train into St Mark's station on the Midland line was in June 1846 and there were great celebrations. Railways had become the chief topic of conversation in Lincoln for some time and there was argument as to where the stations should be. The crossing on the High Street from the Great North station brought complaints that snorting engines alarmed the horses!

66 St Mark's station has a very elegant grey brick symmetrical façade, in Grecian style with a giant Ionic portico, fluted columns and side pavilions. It was built in 1846 by W.A. Nicholson or I.A. Davies as the terminus of the Midland Railway Company's branch line from Nottingham, which was the first railway to be opened in Lincolnshire. The façade of the station has now been incorporated into a new development and excavations in 1986 revealed that it had been built on the site of a Carmelite Friary which was probably founded in 1269.

67 This photograph was taken in the 1900s in front of the ticket agent's office at St Mark's station. It illustrates how the railway opened up opportunities for day trips to the seaside and also longer holidays for the better off. It also shows the part the railways played in the commercial development of Lincoln. Note the advertisement for the distribution of dairy produce and other goods from town to town.

68 Central station, designed by John Henry Taylor of London and completed in 1848, was built on the Great Northern line on St Mary's Street. It is a tudor-style building of grey brick with stone dressings. It culminates in a tower on the left which matches the tower on St Mary le Wigford Church. The Great Northern Railway connected Lincoln to Boston and Peterborough in the south, and Gainsborough and Doncaster in the north. This photograph was taken in 1898 and shows a meeting of Lincoln cyclists in the forecourt of the station.

69 This dramatic picture shows a steam train passing St Mary le Wigford Church and going into Central station. The advert for Virol on the wall brings back memories. In July 1911 the bitterness of a national railway strike erupted in Lincoln when the railway signal box at the Great Northern level crossing was attacked and a rioting crowd smashed windows in the High Street shops.

70 Looking west from Central station we can see a more modern diesel train on the Great Northern line. The history of Lincoln's railway shows that originally there were over 80 projected schemes and a great public meeting was held at the castle which ended in chaos as people could not decide which scheme to support.

71 With the coming of the railways, the growth of industry and the popularity of the races, Lincoln was able to provide some splendid hotels, such as *The Saracen's Head.* The hotel was situated on the left-hand side of the High Street, close to the Stonebow. If we look over the top of the row of shops in line with Ottaker's the Booksellers we can still see the iron balcony and the distinctive windows of the hotel. As we can see from the advertisement, the hotel offered to meet every train with an omnibus, which was an impressive service.

72 As the railway brought more prosperity to the city, so the shops began to develop and Sincil Street was one of the new developments, close to the Great Northern station. Sincil Street was once known as Elder Lane and tradesmen bought vacant sites as a speculative development, many coming from outside Lincoln. These old shops still retain their original character. The photograph taken in 1937 shows Mr. Sowerby proudly showing off some of his excellent pork pies which can still be bought today.

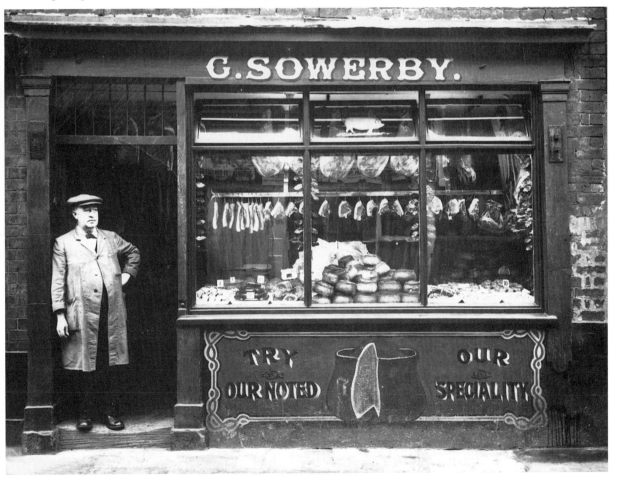

73 *Left.* Lincoln's first photographic studios began to appear in the *Directory* for 1867. Robert Slingsby was one of the first photographers to set up a studio, at 2 Norman Street which is the continuation of St Mary's Street alongside the *Grand Hotel*, until the roads were changed in the 1960s. He later moved to 168 High Street until he was succeeded by another famous photographer Mr. Harrison. Robert Slingsby achieved international fame by winning medals for excellence at the International Exhibition in Paris 1878 and Sidney, Australia in 1879.

74 *Above right.* By 1879 G.A. Howard was advertising in the *Trades Directory* as an Art Photographer. His studio was in Silver Street and he specialised in group views, scenery, machinery and residences. No doubt he was much in demand as industry began to establish itself in Lincoln and manufacturers wished to advertise their products all over the world.

75 *Right.* This aerial view illustrates how Lincoln's engineering industry developed rapidly in the late 1800s, and how workers' housing was built in the industrial area. Waterside cuts through the photograph towards the top. The first three-storied building on the left of Waterside North is the Wellington Foundry, belonging to Fosters. Further along Waterside we can see the Co-operative mills and the power station. Just in front of the power station is the huge Titanic works, owned by Clayton and Shuttleworth's, said to be the length of the ship of that name, and the rest of Clayton's works on Waterside South. Between Waterside and the railway line we see Ruston's works and front right stands Clarke's Crank and Forge and Robey's works.

76 This engraving of Clayton and Shuttleworth's works was produced as part of the official illustrated guide to greet the Great Northern Railway, in 1857. Clayton's building was an impressive sight, now in some need of renovation, standing on Waterside South. Clayton's was an iron foundry established at Stamp End in 1842, producing all kinds of agricultural machinery, including thrashing machines and portable engines, and by the 1860s it was one of the largest engineering works in the world. On the river there are Humber Sloops which were a familiar sight. We can see horses on the towpath— some of the working boats were horse-drawn.

77 Some of the workforce in the early 1900s going home from work. Ruston's eventually gave employment to over 1,600 and overtook Clayton and Shuttleworth as the largest employer in the city. Bicycles were a popular means of transport; otherwise workers walked long distances to and from work. Some workers in the First World War remember walking along Waterside in the tracks made by tanks. In 1857 Joseph Ruston joined the millwright's business of Burton and Proctor, later buying out his partners and expanding the business as the Sheaf Iron Works. When he died in 1897 his firm had produced more than 20,000 steam engines and nearly 11,000 thrashing machines.

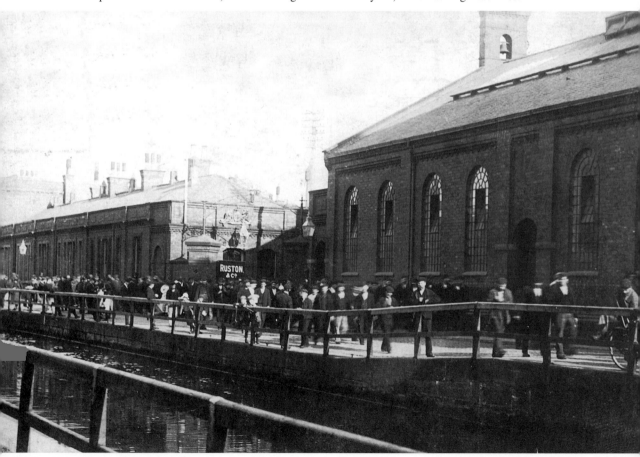

78 More workers, this time going past Clayton and Shuttleworth's at Stamp End. The power station and the Stamp End Lock were familiar features of the landscape.

79 This small bridge, known as Montague Street Bridge, is a familiar sight but not used now. It once carried workers across the river. On the left-hand side of the picture, jutting out is part of the Lincoln Co-operative Mill, which was demolished to make way for Anglian Water Authority offices.

80 Doughty's Oil Crushing Works, along Waterside South, is now being converted into flats. The business was established in the early 1860s by Mr. Charles Doughty, a merchant of bone manure and seed cake in Sincil Street, so that he could produce pure linseed cake. This later became a famous product for feeding cattle. At one time barges would unload their cargoes by means of a bucket system into the silos of the mill. It is a fine building, standing close to what used to be called the Magpie Bridge, now known as Thorn Bridge.

81 This sketch shows a very fine Free Methodist Church which was built on Silver Street in 1865 on the site of the Zion Chapel. The Methodists first met in a lumber room near Gowts Bridge, then a preaching house was opened on Waterside South in 1790. Like the Quakers, the Methodists were considered 'dissenters' and subject to the same restrictions. The Methodist Church split into different branches during the 19th century, including the Free Methodists, but were reunited in 1932.

82 This photograph shows the Lincoln Gasworks, believed to be the Carholme Road site, in Gas Street. The first gasworks was set up on the Brayford in 1828, providing a supply for 76 street lamps and a few private customers. As the business expanded a much larger Gas Works was built beside the railway in Bracebridge and eventually the original works in Carholme Road was turned into a distribution centre. The Gas company was taken over by Lincoln City Council in 1885 which owned it for 60 years until nationalisation.

83 This was one of the electric trams operating on the High Street. The electric tram replaced the horse-drawn tram; tram-sheds (now a car showroom) being located at Bracebridge. Lincoln was the first system to be installed which operated by means of electrified iron studs placed at short intervals between the rails. A battery operated magnet in the tram lifted the studs from below road level to contact with the connecting shoe. *The Great Northern Hotel* stands on the left-hand side of the picture, close to the railway crossing and the station. Note the elegant electric lamps.

84 This postcard shows the method of operating the electric trams. The studs became damaged by tanks and tractors during the First World War and had to be replaced by an overhead cable system in 1919. This photograph was most likely taken during the war and shows both a woman driver and a woman conductor. It was to be many years later before women were to drive the Lincoln City buses. Note the stylish wrought iron surround upstairs and the soldier sitting on the top deck.

85 The High Street as it was in the early 19th century, with citizens making good use of St Mary's Conduit, the medieval water supply.

86 Lincoln from the High Street at the turn of the century, showing the obelisk. Note the coaches that passed through the Stonebow, and the tower of St Peter at Arches before it was moved up to St Giles Estate.

87 The Lincoln Co-operative Society was started by Mr. Thomas Parker, who was a joiner by trade. He brought ideas and principles from Rochdale and Hull and inspired Lincoln people to start a Co-operative Society. The first shop is this one which stood on Napoleon Place, which ran from Norman Place through to Melville Street near the *Grand Hotel*.

88 The Co-op's second shop opened at 1¼ Waterside South, at the back of the present Burton's shop, alongside the High Bridge near to the C & A. Mr. Parker thought that the best way of improving the lives and conditions of his fellow workers was by offering an alternative trading pattern that would assist people. He was concerned at the levels of drinking, having been involved in the Temperance Movement, and thought that by offering alternative interests this might help to keep men from visiting public houses. In 1863 discussion as to whether dividend should be 9d. or 9½d. occupied the general meeting.

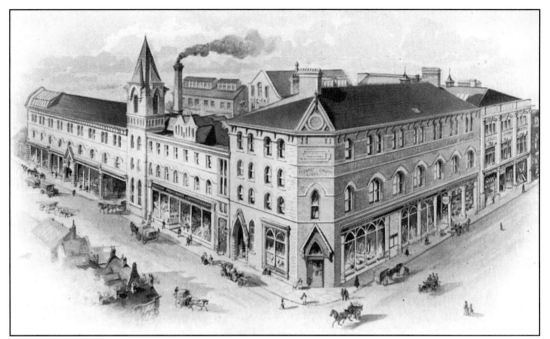

89 The Co-operative Society made great progress and in 1888 the magnificent central premises were designed and opened by Frederick Smith, on the corner of Free School Lane and Silver Street. It was opened with a tea-party and a public meeting in the large hall on the top floor, which could accommodate 1,000 to 1,200 people. The three-storey block in Free School Lane still survives, and was designed for the sale of furniture, crockery, tailoring, boots and shoes. It also had a library and reading rooms which encouraged the working population to widen their horizons. Finds under this building have included skeletons, pottery, roman coins, and tiles.

90 The magnificent Co-operative Mill, built in 1886, stood on Waterside North, opposite the Montague footbridge and Ruston's factory. Unfortunately the mill has now been demolished and new flats have been built. Lincoln has a long history of corn milling and members were keen that the Co-op should build a rolling mill plant. Because there was so much unemployment the Society employed as many of its own members as possible and placed their orders for the mill machinery, engines and boilers with local engineering firms. When it was opened a band played and members marched in a procession led by vehicles laden with bread and flour. The children made deposits in the penny bank and all employees were given tea in the Co-operative Hall.

91 Many small branches and shops were built in Lincoln, including those at Bracebridge, Burton Road, Shakespeare Street, Ripon Street, Canwick Road and Baggholme Road. The Gresham Street shop was No. 10 branch. The building remains as a doctor's surgery, on the corner of Newland Street West.

92 Towards the end of 1891, and because of the rapid development of the lower part of the city where new streets were being constructed off the High Street, the committee thought that it would be advantageous to build a large general store, virtually a sub-central store, with numerous departments. On the day the store was opened 4,800 people were served with tea in the Co-operative Hall, the Drill Hall and the Corn Exchange. The building is still there in the High Street.

93 Shortly after the Society had become established, members expressed a desire to commence a building department which could provide housing on the hire-purchase system. The first grants were for £165 without requiring a deposit from members. Quite a few properties off Monks Road, including these on Hartley Street, were originally Co-operative houses. The department did not fare so well when it won a contract to build the new General Post Office in Guildhall Street. Springs under the ground were struck when excavating work was carried out, which caused a great deal of extra trouble and expense.

94 The Women's Co-operative Guild was formed following a public meeting of the Co-operative Education Committee on 24 October 1888. Women had largely been excluded from public life but began to be included on Boards of Guardians. As their lives were broadened the guild gave them a good training ground for public speaking and promoted the idea of education for women on a par with men. One of the Guild's ideas was for physical training of girls and young women and one of their first projects was to raise the sum of £7 7s. 5d. for gymnasium fittings for a class of young girls. The Guild is still in evidence.

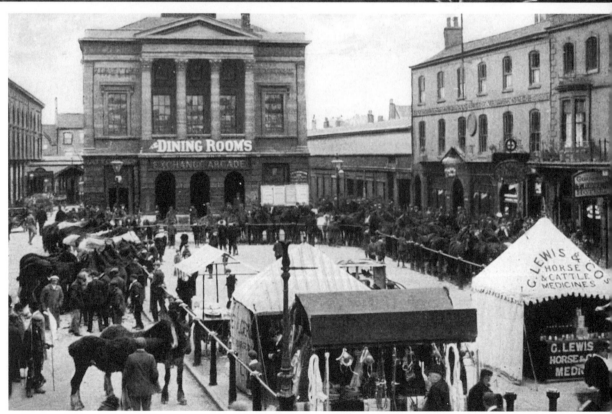

95 *Left*. This interesting postcard shows suffragettes addressing a large crowd in the Cornhill, Lincoln. The large Bass hostelry stood where W.H. Smith's is now. A newspaper account of October 1908 records that 10 suffragettes travelled to Lincoln to shout down the Home Secretary, Herbert Gladstone, where he was speaking at a Liberal meeting in the Corn Exchange. They were pursued through the streets by a hostile, taunting crowd and were on the point of being thrown into the Brayford when Mrs. Cecilia Roberts, wife of the Liberal M.P., intervened to rescue them. They were still brave enough to return the next day and address a crowd in the Cornhill. This may have been the occasion.

96 *Below left*. The large Corn Exchange in the middle of this view had its foundation stone laid in 1847. The new undertaking was under the control of the Lincoln Corn Exchange and Market Company and the building and fixtures cost £12,000. It is recorded that the bells of St Peter's rang out their merriest peals as a procession led by boys of Christ's Hospital made its way to the Cornhill. The larger, newer Corn Exchange was built alongside in 1880. Corn merchants had individual desks and farmers went from desk to desk hoping to strike a good bargain. An old advertisement read: 'Visitors to Lincoln will meet with every accommodation at the celebrated Cornhill Refreshment Rooms: Chops, steaks, soups, etc. at the shortest notice.' The horse fair was held in the High Street at this time and here we see the horses being put through their paces in Cornhill.

97 *Below*. Heavy drinking in the mid-1800s inspired a section of the population to form and promote the Temperance Movement, which was established in 1847. It is said that it inspired Mr. Thomas Parker, founder of the Co-operative Society in Lincoln, as he felt that the working men of Lincoln needed something more to interest them. Citizens and children were urged to sign the pledge and give up the demon drink. Elaborate decorated floats were driven through the streets—this one was turning on to Monks Road. The back of the postcard reads, 'This is a photo of Wesley's part in the procession on Temperance Sunday. They got first prize. Can you see your father on it? I can.'

98 *Left*. A close-up of The Crystal Spring's float. The little boy's banner on his bicycle reads: '3d a day spent on beer is £4.12.3d at the end of the year. Take our advice, give up the drink and buy a bike. What do you think?'

99 *Right*. Caleb Smith of 1 Norman Place was the photographer who took this charming group of young people who featured in Mr. and Mrs. Will Gadsby's fairy choir. Many of Lincoln's elders remember the choir, who entertained at the Temperance Hall and other halls. The Temperance Hall was later to become the Central Hall which stood on the site of Thorngate House in St Swithin's Square.

100 *Below*. The Arboretum was built as another distraction for the drinkers of Lincoln and must have been a splendid place for families to enjoy. It was designed by Edward Milner in 1868 and opened in 1872. It had plants and birds for people to admire and was planted with quite rare trees. The Victorian cast-iron bandstand was well used for all sorts of public occasions and festivals. The lion is a special statue which was once painted in red, yellow and black stripes, causing much speculation. This photograph was taken in the 1930s.

SHEAF WORKS PRIZE BAND. LINCOLN.

Belmont House, Lincoln.

MISS BACON

RECEIVES a limited number of **YOUNG LADIES** to BOARD and EDUCATE. The advantages she offers are a thorough personal, practical acquaintance with all that is desirable for the TUITION and TRAINING of YOUNG LADIES; the assistance of the best Masters and Professors, and the Preparation of Young Ladies for the OXFORD and CAMBRIDGE LOCAL EXAMINATIONS, when desirable. In this, her Establishment is pre-eminent in the County; three-fourths of the Pupils sent from it, for Examination, passed most successfully; an excellent proof of the merits of her system.

MISS BACON begs a careful perusal of her Synopsis and Prospectus, which will be forwarded on application, with every information as to Terms, &c., which are moderate; and there are *no* Day Pupils.

BELMONT HOUSE is a large and comfortable Establishment, pleasantly situated on the Hill, in the most salubrious position in Lincolnshire, and commands a beautiful and extensive view.

101 *Left*. Each works had a football team and a band. Here is Ruston's Sheaf Works prize band, standing in front of the elegant conservatory on the upper terrace of the Arboretum, now sadly gone.

102 *Below left*. This photograph is marked as Lincoln School—1857-75. It was taken in 1861 outside the Headmaster's House, now part of St Joseph's School. It was known as the Lincoln Grammar School which originated in Greyfriars. The main school building was built in 1884, designed by William Watkins. This building is described by Pevsner as a hall like a small City of London Hall of the 17th century, with a cupola. By 1868 there were 15 public schools catering for over 5,000 children and 42 private schools accommodating 1,065 children. This school was headed by an imposing headmaster. Boys wear distinctive caps, boaters and even a couple of top hats.

103 *Above*. Girl's education was more limited and this advertisement was obviously aimed at wealthy young ladies. The curriculum appears to have been on a par with the boys' private schools as it does offer preparation for Oxford and Cambridge Local Examinations.

104 *Below*. The Girl's Grammar School was founded in 1873 and housed in a red terracotta building, which was later occupied by Lincoln College of Art and De Montford University, on Lindum Hill. The building was designed by William Watkins. Some of the girls in their distinctive uniforms can be seen wandering in the grounds which was known as the Temple Gardens. We can also see the pretty Greek-style temple, copied from the Choragic Monument of Thrasyllus. There is a figure of Niobe on the parapet. Remains of the temple are behind the Usher Gallery.

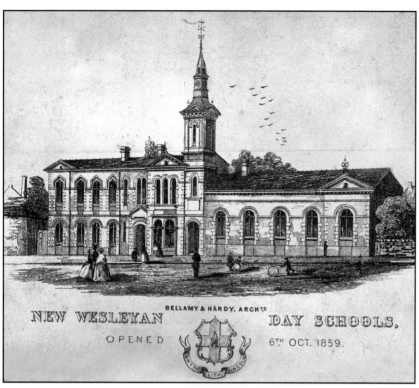

NEW WESLEYAN DAY SCHOOLS,

OPENED 6TH OCT. 1859.

BELLAMY & HARDY, ARCHTS

105 Down Rosemary Lane still stands the fine red and white brick Wesleyan Day School, as shown in this architect's impression by Bellamy and Hardy. The school has a tall thin tower and cupola. The building was erected in 1859 and divided into boys, girls and infants. It was said at the time to be the largest educational establishment in Lincolnshire, providing accommodation for 600 children. It regularly had 638 on the books and an average weekly attendance of 500 in 1864, which was high. It served the children in the surrounding area and indicates the massive building programme at that time.

106 The infants' department at Rosemary Lane Wesleyan Day School in the early 1900s. The picture shows a suprising collection of toys including a doll's house; a cat; an elephant as well as dolls and a doll's bed, which illustrates how well the school was equipped at the time.

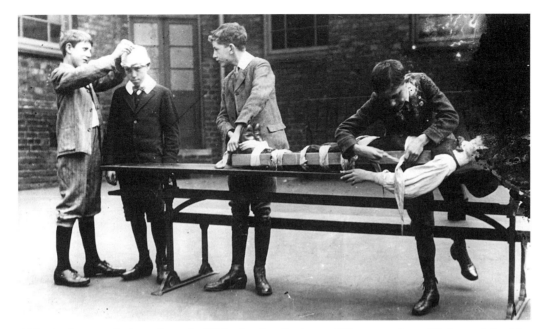

107 A photograph from the early 1900s showing the boys of Rosemary Lane Wesleyan School in a first-aid class. The school was notable for its covered play area and drawing room for the boys, with also a dining room, hot water central heating and gas lighting. The view from the master's house covered the entire playground.

108 A delightful picture of the girls of St Botolph's School also taken in the 1900s. The girls are wearing smocks, black stockings and highly polished boots. Most of them have long hair, but the girl in the foreground has hers shorn.

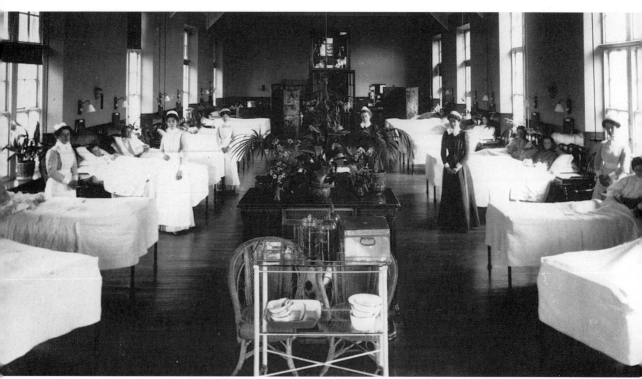

109   The County Hospital was built in Sewell Road in 1878, the foundation stone being laid by Lord Brownlow. This rather formal pose in the women's ward reflects the orderly regime which the nurses would have followed. By 1907 it provided 120 beds and a newly equipped operating theatre with the latest electrical and sterilising appliances. A nursing home was added in 1914 and an X-Ray Department in 1922. A laboratory was installed as a war memorial. Nursing gave women opportunities to make a career for themselves outside the home.

110   The children's ward was added by 1907 and again we see the formal pose for the photographer. One of the girls is holding an interesting life-sized doll. There seem to be two children in the cot at the front but this may have just been for the photograph.

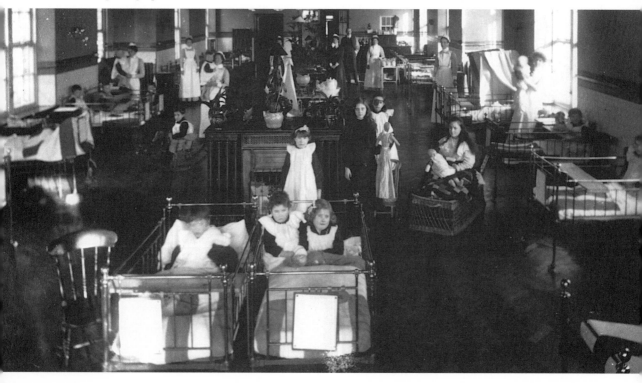

111 Lincoln has an interesting theatrical history. The Palace Theatre, managed by Mr. Dobney, stood on Newland, at the corner of Orchard Street, and began life in 1871 as the Masonic Hall. The masons then sold the hall to the Colan brothers who presented stage shows. In 1901 the theatre was reopened as the Empire Music Hall by Councillor George Beagle, whose initials decorated the heavy red velvet curtains. In 1901 the Empire Music Hall presented Victoria Monks in 'Won't you come home Bill Bailey'. Ticket prices for the balcony and side galleries were 3d., stalls were 2d., and the wooden benches in the gods, 4d. It became the Plaza Cinema until it was destroyed by an incendiary bomb in 1943.

112 The Lincoln Theatre, later re-named the Grand Electric Cinema, at 262 High Street was originally an 18th-century residence. In 1913 the Grand Electric installed the first film combined with sound; a forerunner of the 'talkies'. It was Lincoln's second cinema to open. The variety format of the Music Hall provided a convenient way of showing early cinematic films which could be inserted into a bill of live entertainment. The cinema operated until 1960, when it closed with the film 'Gigi'.

113 Horse racing first occurred on Lincoln Heath, south of the city. After the enclosure act, it moved out to Welton, then on to the Carholme. The Lincoln Handicap was first run in 1849 over a two-mile stretch, later reduced to a mile and a half, then in 1864 to a mile. The grandstand was erected in 1897 by William Mortimer and Son. It had cast-iron columns and was asymmetrical. The races attracted thousands of people to Lincoln and it was a sad decision when the Horse Race Betting Board decided not to allocate fixtures to Lincoln after 1965, despite appeals and protests. The last meeting took place in 1964. The other two stands have now disappeared—it would be good to see an imaginative use made of the remaining grandstand which is an evocative reminder of our past.

114 In 1936 the races were thriving and big names in the racing world came from all over the country. This photograph was taken by an enthusiastic amateur, Mr. D.S. Glover, who kept a record that the jockey on No. 3 was Fred Stephens and No. 8 Prior. The race was the Gautby selling plate and the two jockeys were captured leaving the saddling enclosure.

115 In 1905 a tragedy struck Lincoln when a typhoid epidemic devastated the city. As a result over 1,000 people contracted the disease and 131 people died. It was discovered that the water supply was contaminated and in spite of many protests to the Lincoln Corporation it was to be another 10 years before a new supply was found. People had to queue for their water. The people waiting here were on Burton Road and the water is contained in water carts brought around by J. Harrison, carrier, on behalf of Lincon Corporation. The photographer was Hickingbotham, Lincoln.

116 A re-enactment of the epidemic took place in Lincoln in 1987 in the form of a community play entitled 'A Bucket Full of Daisies'. The period was carefully researched and the words used in the play were, as far as possible, *verbatim*. Authentic costumes had to reflect Lincoln people at the turn of the century.

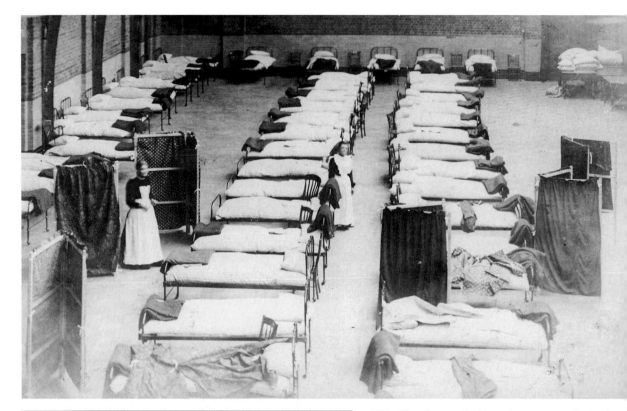

Why not boil them for Ten – minutes in their own water

117 The first typhoid patients were admitted to the Dixon ward at the County Hospital. This soon became full and patients then occupied the new Infectious Diseases Hospital at St George's. When this hospital became full, other halls had to be put into use and the Drill Hall was the largest of these. We can see a Bromhead nurse in the picture surrounded by about one hundred beds.

118 This was a hilarious cartoon drawn in 1905 by a Lincoln artist, A.E. White, in which members of Lincoln Corporation were immersed in a cauldron of boiling water. The caption read 'Why not boil them for ten minutes in their own water', which reflected the anger which citizens felt as they realised that the corporation were dragging their feet when it came to providing a new water supply. The original cartoon was displayed in the shop window of fruiterer Mr. Fred Burkitt on West Parade, on the corner of Orchard Street opposite the police station, and attracted large crowds.

119 This delightful photograph was taken in 1910 showing young women swimming and diving in the Witham, in a spot known locally as 'The Goshes'. The Witham was a popular place for bathing at the turn of the century. It was not realised that there could be health hazards and that effluents from industrial establishments could contain harmful substances.

120 This postcard shows floods on Sincil Bank which occurred in December 1910. Note that in those days there were no railings on either side of the bank. Although the first victims of the typhoid epidemic came from the uphill area, there were extra hazards experienced by people who lived beside the drains.

121 The new water supply eventually arrived from the pumping station at Elkesley, Nottinghamshire. There were great celebrations which began with a service in the cathedral. This was a commemorative postcard issued at the time. A procession made its way to the Arboretum, where the fountain was switched on and the water spurted up to the heavens. One Lincoln woman recalled, 'We couldn't drink enough of it, it was lovely. It was like ice, it was really nice'.

122 The very fine water tower on West gate was built and opened as part of Lincoln's new water supply in 1911, following the typhoid outbreak. It was designed by Sir Reginald Blomfield and has been mistaken for the real keep of the castle. One visitor enquired whether it was a Roman tower. The water tank is carried on a circular brick tower within a square outer tower faced in brown Darley Dale gritstone.

123 This is still a familiar shop to many people in Lincoln. It stands on Bailgate and is a fruit and vegetable shop now owned and run by Mrs. Meldrum. Mr. Brummitt used to send his poultry all over the country. The postcard was posted in 1906.

124 Another very fine shop which was a familiar sight on the High Street. Interestingly enough, it remained a fish shop as it was taken over by Macfisheries in the 1930s, only closing in the late 1970s. Mr. Cooper was also an ice-merchant and delivered ice to other fish merchants and ice-cream vendors in the Lincoln area.

125 Lincoln saw many processions enjoyed by the people of the city. Many were held in the Arboretum. This one was held for the lifeboat on Saturday, 12 June 1909 and the procession seems to be going down Baggholme Road.

126 This is how Brayford Pool Basin looked in the early 1900s. The *Lincoln Directory* for 1887 lists the buildings as follows: Just out of the picture on the right-hand side stood Dickinson's Flour Mill, then Peel Bros. Corn Merchants office and warehouse. Swanpool Court runs alongside this building and next to this was Patterson & Son's Silk Mill, then Clarke, W. & Son, coal office, later named Goole Haulage Co. Ltd. From the *Black Bull Inn* yard stood E. Nelson's office and warehouse; F.E. Holland, corn warehouse, Goodbarne, W.S. Builder, *Crown Hotel*, M. Pheasant, Melbourne Bros. stores. We can see G.H. Pacey's warehouse and in front of this the old swing bridge that has sadly disappeared. A magnificent Humber Sloop is moored which would have come down from the Humber with its load.

127 The cattle and sheep market moved to Monks Road in the area now occupied by North Lincs College in 1849. The original sheep fair had taken place in St Swithin's Square. The sheep fair in Lincoln was one of the most important in England and at its busiest up to 70,000 sheep were bought and sold.

128 This postcard gives a good view of the magnificent Longwool sheep famous in Lincolnshire. The original sheep fair was granted by Charles II, commencing on the second Tuesday in April and lasting four days. This fair included the horse fair. By the time this postcard was taken in the 1900s, it had been transferred to the West Common, clearly identified by the row of trees alongside the Carholme Road. Sadly, it ceased altogether in 1941.

129 This is Lincoln Fair after it had moved in 1872 to the Cheviot Close on the site of the cattle market on Monks Road. The fair was attended by enterprising showmen and traders and contained bazaars, menageries, monstrosities, ghost shows, boxing booths and peep shows which are remembered with delight by some of Lincoln's older citizens. This postcard shows a carousel on the left-hand side, and a huge steam engine which powered the machinery, and there are donkeys waiting to give rides.

130 In 1907 Lincoln was chosen to host the Royal Show, which was held on the West Common. Lincoln was decorated in lavish fashion—this view is looking north up the High Street. The arch spanned the road between Peacock Willson's Bank on the west side and the *Queen's Hotel* on the east. Now a pizza restaurant and until recently the Electricity Board occupy these sites; just through the arch can be seen Barclays Bank. The arch had a Ruston's portable engine on top, flanked by ploughs, the whole display portraying the wealth of Lincoln's industries. The photograph was taken by P. Jones of 66 High Street, one of the leading Lincoln photographers of the time.

131 The Royal Show was visited by King Edward VII, accompanied by the Grand Duke of Hesse and Prince Albert of Greece, on 26 June 1907. The Royal Party came up the High Street, turned along Guildhall Street and drove along Newland to the West Common. The row of shops and houses on the right-hand side of Newland was demolished to make way for Newland Health Centre. There is a gas lamp in the foreground. Programmes for the event cost 2s. 6d. The typhoid epidemic was easing at this time and the event no doubt helped Lincoln people to feel better.

132 This photograph taken in 1910 shows the High Street looking comparatively quiet. Lincoln's fine buildings are still a familiar part of the landscape. The one on the right was by William Watkins, now Dolcis shoes.

133 Steep Hill, with its little shops that have always been of interest to the visitor. The opening on the left-hand side of the picture is St Martin's Lane and the pump on the right-hand side is still there on the corner of Well Lane.

134 Just before the outbreak of the First World War a very fine building was erected on Free School Lane—the Public Library presented by Mr. Carnegie. The building was designed by Sir Reginald Blomfield who also built the Usher Gallery and the water tower on Westgate. He remarked that the dome was not merely ornamental but marked the importance of the library building. The library signified the growth of adult education in Lincoln; societies such as the Workers Education Association had been established in 1911. A new library has recently been opened, keeping the façade of the Carnegie building.

135 The old barracks on Burton Road is perhaps better known now as the home of the Museum of Lincolnshire Life, but this photograph was apparently taken on the day before the squadron was called up to go to the First World War. The message on the back reads: 'The whole squadron the day before we left there. Major Royds is the centre figure in the front'. The barracks was designed by Henry Goddard in 1857. There is a contemporary row of terraced houses in Mill Row behind the barracks.

136 The troops were assembled on the race-course, in front of the Grandstand, when the army was called up to go to fight in the First World War. Sadly 971 men and one woman lost their lives in the war, and Lincoln saw many changes over the course of the war years.

137 & 138   One of the many changes was in the engineering works in Lincoln. Lincoln was well placed to produce munitions and aeroplanes during the war, and became one of the leading producers of planes in the country. Ruston Proctor and Company received their first order from the War Office in January 1915 and a special factory was built beside the Witham at Boultham. During the war women replaced men in the engineering works and in Fig. 137 they are working in the wing erection and covering bay. Women stretched and sewed the canvas on to the wings—the next process was to cover them with dope to tighten and strengthen them. Robey's built about 300 aircraft and Clayton and Shuttleworth's built Sopwith Camels in their huge Titanic works. Below is Ruston's 1,000th plane.

139 *Above*. This was a Robey's plane, a Short 184 N2900, which was a two-seater torpedo bomber and reconnaisance floatplane. It was brought to the Great Northern station yard to raise money for the Red Cross. Note on the right-hand side Walker's Studio, in Norman Place. Walker was a leading photographer at the time.

140 *Below*. The aircraft were tested on the West Common which became known as No. 4 Aircraft Acceptance Park. The hangars were camouflaged sheds situated on the site of the tennis courts. Later two more hangars were built alongside Alderman's Walk, and these were supplemented by five Bessoneau sheds (canvas covered)—one opposite the Grandstand and four at the end of West Parade.

141 *Above right*. This photograph shows one of the hangars with the second Ruston built aeroplane—B.E.2c 2671—standing in front of it. This plane was test-flown by Captain Tennant making an initial half-hour flight and delivered to Farnborough by air on 18 July 1915. Captain Tennant, with a passenger, left the West Common and followed the railway line for London. He got lost and landed in a field in Sandy, Bedfordshire to enquire the way. The farmer gave them lunch and they finally arrived at Farnborough at 7p.m.

142 *Right*. Women munition workers from Ruston's enjoying an outing in the Arboretum.

143 Ruston workers, both men and women, seen here with some of their engines. Note the railway track at the front. A light railway ran in front of the works in order to move goods and machinery.

144 Not only did women take the place of men in the engineering works but they also formed women's football teams for the firms. This was Ruston Ladies 1st Team. Mrs. Sherriff, who owns the original picture says that her aunt, Ethel Webster, was in the team, working on aircraft in the First World War. These women look pretty tough opponents—it is interesting that women's football still has difficulty in being accepted.

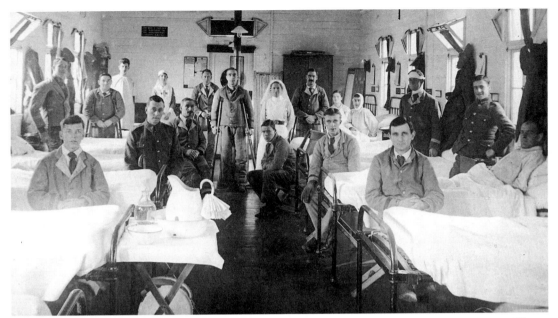

145 During the First World War, Christ's Hospital School was used as the 4th Northern Military Hospital, which housed the war wounded. These men were looked after in huts at the back of the school.

146 Eventually a war memorial was unveiled to mark the lives of those lost in the First World War. There were three attempts to raise money for the memorial which was finally unveiled on 25 October 1922 by Sir W.R. Robertson. The monument was designed by Montague A. Hall, a Lincoln architect, and is a favourite spot for people to gather outside St Benedict's Church. We can see the overhead cables of the electric tramway which eventually replaced the special stud-type system, see Fig. 84. The new overhead system was put into place in 1919.

Unveiling of Lincoln War Memorial by Sir W. R. Robertson

147 Swanpool estate is a fine example of forward thinking by one of the main engineering firms in Lincoln, on land acquired and built on by Ruston's. Soon after the First World War in 1919 it was decided to lay out a garden suburb and designers were engaged who had helped to build a similar scheme at Letchworth. Only part of the scheme was built, comprising 113 houses. The occupants enjoyed spacious houses in wide pleasant avenues, which has been made into a conservation area.

148 Does this bring back memories? These are the horses and proud workers who drove the Lincoln Corporation dustcarts. Note how the horse brasses are polished. The yard was opposite the Westgate water tower on Chapel Lane. It eventually closed in the 1960s. The refuse was taken to the Corporation Refuse Destructor, erected in 1915 to destroy the whole of the refuse daily, the steam generated to be used for operating the sewage pumps. The last horse retired to Manor Farm, Canwick, in the 1950s-60s; the farmer also looking after the sewage works.

149 A big advancement. A later picture of the Corporation refuse collectors on what looks like a newly laid out St Giles estate. Now they are the proud drivers of a Lincoln-made Clayton's electric wagon. Clayton's ran a subsidiary company called Clayton Wagons Ltd., which was formed to specialise in steam and electric road wagons, and this must have been one of their vehicles.

150 After the First World War, times were hard for Lincoln's industries because of the general world-wide slump and, in particular, the loss of the Russian market, due to the revolution and British support for the forces opposed to the Bolshevik regime. By 1923 Ruston's were obliged to cut their labour force from 13,000 to 4,750. It is said that men spent their time polishing their machines; perhaps this is illustrated in this picture.

151 The Usher Gallery was designed by Sir Reginald Blomfield and opened in 1927 on the Temple Gardens. It is striking mainly because it stands in a magnificent position overlooking the city and away from other buildings. James Ward Usher was born in 1845, the elder son of James Usher, jeweller and watchmaker, in the High Street. The younger James joined the business in 1860 and chose the Lincoln Imp as a suitable novelty for visitors. His collection formed the nucleus of items in the Gallery.

52 *Left.* This postcard shows HRH the Prince of Wales when he visited Lincoln, possibly to open the Usher Gallery in 1927. We can see the *Saracen's Head* and the Midland Bank on the corner of the High Street. The photograph appears to have been taken from the window of the Guildhall.

53 *Below.* This photograph, taken in the 1930s, shows Brayford Wharf North and the Hovis Mills, which have now disappeared, once known as the Albion mills. One mill produced the special flour needed to bake the famous Hovis bread. Beyond the small Hovis building is the Electricity House with the original works of 1899 at the back. This building is still standing. Beyond that is the Lincoln Co-operative dairy and butchery. Alongside the Co-op was a three-storey 19th-century maltings built by Bass and beyond this the premises of C.W. Green, Marine Engineering, previously a malthouse and grain warehouse.

154a *Above.* A rare panoramic view of Lincoln photographed from the top of the Drill Hall on Broadgate in the early 1930s. On the left of the picture we see Unity Square and the Oddfellows Hall buildings with Shipley's on the corner; the area is now occupied by a garage and multi-storey car-park. All the houses and courts have been demolished.

154b *Below*. St Rumbold Street and the original Foster's Wellington Works on Waterside North. As we look down Broadgate we can see how the road narrowed, where the present offices of Ruston's and the telephone exchange stand. On the right-hand side of the picture we see St Swithin's Church, behind which stood the Central Hall.

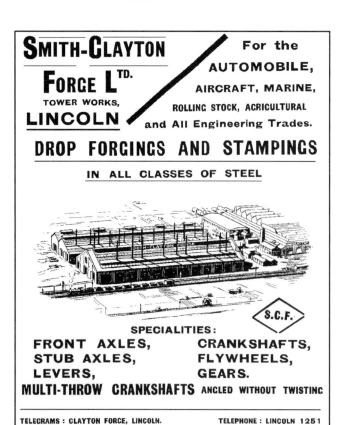
155 *Left*. In the 1930s Clayton and Shuttleworth's went into liquidation and the forge was sold to Smith's of Coventry and became known as Smith Clayton Forge Ltd. At this time they were still manufacturing parts for aircraft, automobiles and marine craft.

156 *Below*. Another part of Clayton's became known as Clayton Dewandre Co. Ltd., and the picture shows the Servo Brake Machine Bay in the huge Titanic works. At that time the machine bay was still equipped with overhead belting systems.

157 *Above.* This is a rare picture of the inside of Clarke's Crank and Forge factory which was founded in 1859, next to Robey's works. The company specialised in crank-shafts. Shown in the picture is a steam forging-press known as the Davy Steam Hydraulic Intensifier, which had the power of 1,200 tons and was served by two electric travelling cranes which had capacities of 30 and 10 tons.

158 Part of this fertilizer factory still remains along the Carholme Road, out towards Saxilby. Doughty's Oil Mill joined with Richardson to form this factory which manufactured compound fertilisers.

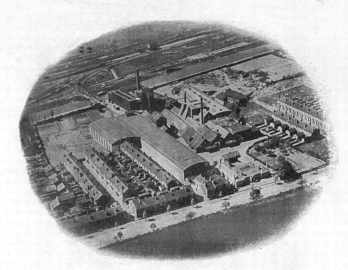

SINGLETON, FLINT & CO., LTD.
NEWLAND WORKS, LINCOLN

ESTABLISHED 1803.   Telegrams—"SINGLETON, LINCOLN."

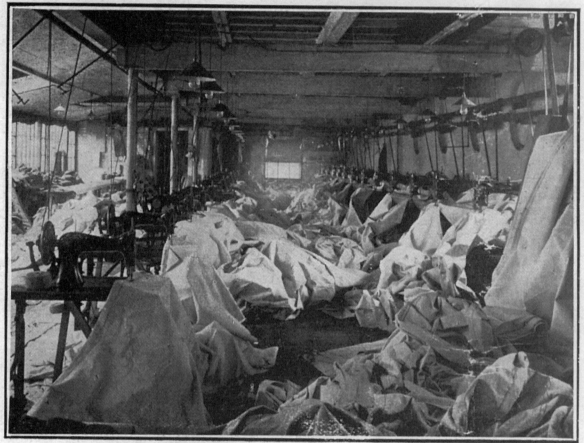

Section of Power Machine Sewing Room at Newland Works.

WHOLESALE of MANUFACTURERS
WATERPROOF COVERS
FOR TRANSPORT AND
ALL PURPOSES

ALSO ASK FOR **BRUSHES**
OUR NOTED

AS GOOD AS A. ROOF

TRADE **BACME** MARK

BINDER CANVASES FOR ALL MAKES OF BINDERS

159 This factory was owned by Singleton, Flint & Co. Ltd., and was situated opposite the *Vine* public house on Newland Street West. The company started by making tarpaulins for transport purposes. The building has now gone and new housing has been built on the site.

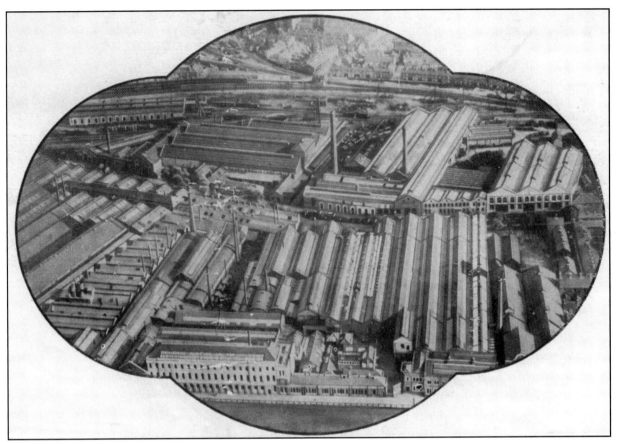

160 An advertisement for Ruston and Hornsbys in the 1930s.

161 Ruston Bucyrus was formed and took over the manufacture of a complete range of diesel or electric excavators. The range included shovels, draglines, skimmers, grabbing cranes and cranes for use on excavating and material handling work.

162 This crane was a familiar sight on Brayford Head. Here it can be seen helping to unload a piece of machinery from a dredger used for clearing out Brayford Pool in the 1930s.

163 The Butter Market façade now forms the centre-piece of the Central Market on Waterside South. Originally the building stood alongside St Peter at Arches Church opposite Binns and just beyond the C. & A. Stores.

164 When the Second World War broke out, bombers became a familiar sight above Lincoln. By 1941 Hampdens and Manchesters were largely replaced by Lancasters and by April 1945 a force of 700 Lancaster bombers was flying. In more peaceful times the people of Lincoln are occasionally able to see the Lancasters and Spitfires flying over Lincoln.

165 During the Second World War women were again brought back into the works and here they are seen painting one of the Ruston tanks that was to be be sent to Russia. Mrs. Martin of Bracebridge Heath was one of the painters.

166 A line of tanks ready for transportation being pulled by a Ruston engine on the light railway running alongside Cannon Glue Factory. This building still remains on Firth Road.

167 Some of the women worked in the Light Core Making Shop. There is a Core Blowing Machine in the left foreground. The work was definitely not for the faint-hearted.

168 & 169 *Left and below left*. The women in the Core Shop got very dirty; one woman said that the cores were made of cow dung, straw and black lead. She could still remember the smell and that the women wore jackets and boiler suits with bibs and braces. Fig. 168 shows 'Lil' working in the Core Shop.

170 *Below right*. Another woman working alongside the men in the 'Fettling' Shop.

171 There was much rejoicing when the war eventually came to an end, although for many people there came a great readjustment to their lives. These Lincoln mothers and children have been attending a special ceremony of Thanksgiving and are posing for a photograph outside the Central Library. People were asked to support Thanksgiving Week and urged to Keep on Saving. This is quite a contrast to life in the 1990s when spending has been encouraged.

172 1947 saw a further Royal Show in Lincoln which again most likely helped to revive spirits after the war. This was attended by King George VI and Queen Elizabeth. This souvenir bus ticket was issued for the special occasion.

173 Children bathing in the open-air baths, probably at some time in the 1940s. These were known as the Wickham Garden Baths; originally a reservoir to serve uphill Lincoln and later the overflow system to serve the water tower on Westgate. They have now been covered in and used for bowling, but a clue to their whereabouts can be found by the street name Reservoir Street off the Burton Road.

174 The present Lincoln City Football Club was founded in 1883, subsequently moving to Sincil Bank ground in 1884. In 1892 the team turned professional and was chosen that year with 12 other clubs to form the second division of the Football League. It remained in this division until 1920. It won promotion in 1947-8, 1951-2, 1975-6 and 1980-1. This lively photograph shows Lincoln City footballers leap-frogging in 1948—they look in good spirits; perhaps due to their success.

175 The Coronation train seen in Lincoln Central station in 1953.

176 The 1960s and '70s brought many changes to the layout of Lincoln, including the Pelham Bridge development. The roundabout featured in this photograph was a feature before the new road system was put into operation on Melville Street.

177 The 1980s saw the Waterfront Shopping Centre, which fitted well into the Waterside North scheme. The footbridge was built in 1957 and replaced an older bridge which was locally called the Mayfield Bridge, built in 1868 through the activities of a Mr. Walker, a baker on Waterside South, and a Mr. Mayfield, who had a boot and shoe shop on the opposite bank.

178 A present-day photograph which illustrates the pleasure visitors feel as they walk up and down the still cobbled steep hill, full of fascinating little shops. Most of these buildings can be traced to medieval times.

179 The obelisk which now stands in the newly created St Mark's Square looks very much like a new monument. In fact it dates from 1762-63 and was built as a water conduit by Gale of Hull. Restored in 1863, it was dedicated as the Albert Fountain after the Prince Consort. It was originally situated on the east side of High Bridge overlooking the River Witham. Its water supply was fed from springs on Monks Road. It was dismantled in 1939 and put into storage, then brought out again in 1996 and reconstructed in the St Mark's development.

180 A 1996 aerial photograph of Brayford Pool having been cleared for the building of the new university.

181 Our story begins and ends with the Brayford Pool, since in 1996 the University of Lincolnshire was built on the edge of the pool, perhaps very close to the original settlement of the Iron-Age people. The new bridge to link Tritton Road with Carholme Road was completed and opened in 1997. The bridge opened up new vistas of the cathedral. Visitors and citizens of Lincoln cannot fail to be stirred as they look across this magnificent stretch of water and perhaps reflect on all that has gone before.

Bibliography

Beckwith, Ian, *The Book of Lincoln*, Barracuda (1990)

Bennett, S and N., *An Historical Atlas of Lincs*, The University of Hull Press (1993)

Bray, C., Grantham, K., Wright, A., *The Enemy in our Midst. The Story of Lincoln's Typhoid Epidemic*, K.M. Associates, Lincoln (1905)

Clarke, G., *Cinemas of Lincoln*, Mercia Cinema Society (1991)

Hill, Francis, Sir, *Georgian Lincoln*, CUP (1966)

Hill, Francis, Sir, *Medieval Lincoln*, CUP (1965)

Hill, Francis, Sir, *A Short History of Lincoln*, Lincoln Civic Trust (1979)

Hurt, Fred, *Lincoln During the War* (1991)

Jones, Michael J., *Lincoln—History and Guide*, Alan Sutton Publishing Ltd. (1993)

Melton, B.L., *One Hundred and Fifty Years at the Lawn*

Newman, Bernard, *One Hundred Years of Good Company*

Pevsner, N., *Lincolnshire* (1989)

Mills, D.R. (ed.), *20th Century Lincolnshire*, Vol. XII, History of Lincs (1989)

Whitwell, J.B., *Roman Lincolnshire* (1970) History of Lincs Local History Society

The Story of Lincoln Co-operative Society (1904)

Wright, N., *Lincolnshire Towns and Industries, 1700-1914*, Vol. XI, History of Lincs (1982)

Index

Roman numerals refer to pages in the introduction and arabic numerals to individual illustrations.